Praise for *So L*

"Laura has been a friend of mine fo[...]
story of love and hope and Jesus. As you read these pages you are going
to laugh, you are going to cry, and best of all, you are going to think."

—Bob Goff
Author and speaker; Sweet Maria's husband, dad
of several kids, and grandpa of a couple more

"Change, upheaval, and tough transitions. They're God's favorite way
of shaking you up and out of what's 'normal.' Yes, it's hard, but it's
necessary if we are to grow in grace. My friend Laura Story speaks to
this beautifully and powerfully in her wonderful new book, *So Long,
Normal*, and I give her work a double thumbs-up! Read it and you'll
understand why saying goodbye to 'normal' is your passport to a faith-
filled life of surprise and adventure."

—Joni Eareckson Tada
Joni and Friends International Disability Center

"With a lightness of touch akin to her piano playing, Laura Story helps
us to stay steady in a world turned upside down."

—Alistair Begg
Senior pastor Parkland Church, Cleveland, Ohio

"Laura is a voice I trust, so much so that I invite her to join me every
chance I can at Fresh Grounded Faith. And this book is another affir-
mation of why I love her! It's a guidebook for navigating the unknown
written by one who has traveled that land herself. So if you're struggling
to feel secure in an uncertain world, Laura's wise and gentle voice is
for you."

—Jennifer Rothschild
Author and founder, Fresh Grounded Faith Events

So Long, Normal

Also by Laura Story

What If Your Blessings Come Through Raindrops?
When God Doesn't Fix It: Lessons You Never Wanted
to Learn, Truths You Can't Live Without
I Give Up: The Secret Joy of a Surrendered Life

So Long, Normal

WITHDRAWN

Living and Loving the Free Fall of Faith

Laura Story

with Bill Wood

W PUBLISHING GROUP

AN IMPRINT OF THOMAS NELSON

So Long, Normal

Published in Nashville, Tennessee, by W Publishing, an imprint of Thomas Nelson.

Thomas Nelson titles may be purchased in bulk for educational, business, fund-raising, or sales promotional use. For information, please email SpecialMarkets@ThomasNelson.com.

ISBN 978-0-7852-4861-3 (audiobook)
ISBN 978-0-7852-4857-6 (eBook)
ISBN 978-0-7852-4852-1 (TP)

Library of Congress Cataloging-in-Publication Data

Library of Congress Control Number: 2021937078

Printed in the United States of America

21 22 23 24 25 LSC 10 9 8 7 6 5 4 3 2 1

To Martin, Josie, Ben, Griffin, and Timothy—
Our lives have been anything but normal, but I wouldn't
miss this adventure for anything in the world!

Contents

CONTENTS

The Truth About Normal

The church where I work has an adventure treetop ropes course. I know, it's kind of bizarre. When I first started working there, I noticed the shiny steel wire crossing over a massive swimming pool and assumed the church had some crazy way of doing baptisms. But I soon discovered that Presbyterians use less water when baptizing, not more.

The zip line had been built for the church's camp ministry, which serves thousands of kids every summer, teaching them the truths of the gospel in a fun, engaging way. Honestly, I didn't really care what they used it for, as long as I never was required to do it! I like the ground. And I especially like when my feet are firmly planted on it. But sure enough, I got that dreaded email one day: *Staff Team-Building Opportunity.*

My coworkers and I would be going through the ropes course in an effort to bond, or something like that. And it was mandatory.

I hadn't signed up for this.

I put on my bravest face and headed out to "bond" with my team. I'm pretty outdoorsy anyway. What could go wrong? The first few exercises were easy, including a trust fall and a small rock-climbing wall. But our last challenge? You guessed it. The dreaded zip line. As I crawled up to the tower using the cargo net, many things ran through my mind. *I'm unbelievably out of shape. Would it have killed me a do a few push-ups over the past few years?*

As I ascended higher, the ground—my good old friend—seemed to be leaving me. *Should I have made a will like my parents encouraged me to do? Is it more probable I'll die from shock or the impact of my body splatting on the pavement?* Many such thoughts rolled around in my head as I climbed to the top of the sixty-foot platform. By the time I made it, my whole body was shaking.

At the top, a young man with a kind voice greeted me. "Are you ready for this?"

I wanted to smack him. *Are you seriously asking me this right now?!* But considering there was no easy alternative way to get back down, and my life was literally in his hands, I kept my mouth shut and just smiled. While connecting my rope lanyard to the 1,350-foot line, he noticed my anxiety. Perhaps what gave it away was the tears welling up in my eyes, or the trembling from head to toe, or the way I was gripping the poor guy's arm so tightly he was no doubt losing circulation in his right hand. Whatever it was, I will never forget his words prior to gently nudging me off the platform.

"Laura," he said, "I could tell you that this zip line can hold up to five thousand pounds, but that's not going to reassure you. The step you are about to take requires courage. And having courage isn't about the absence of fear. It's acknowledging that fear and being willing to take the next step anyway."

So long, normal.

Friends, at this point I feel like I need to be honest with you. My name is Laura, and I am not a normal person to begin with. As I say this, it feels as though I am introducing myself in a support group, but I want you to know for at least a couple of reasons. First, as you read this book you will quickly discover that this claim is not my attempt at humor. Second, anyone who knows me already knows I am not normal. It's not a well-kept secret.

For those of you who are new friends, let me give you a quick snapshot. I am a musician, a member of that free-spirited sect of individuals known for their eclectic quirks and abnormalities. I am also a Christian. This means, in a sense, I am a person with dual citizenship. I am a citizen of the here and now, and I am a citizen of what is often described as an upside-down kingdom. A kingdom that is already and not yet. Confusing enough? It gets even more interesting.

I am married to a man with a disability, and we have four children. Vocationally, I work at a church the first half of every week, then jump on a plane and travel to speaking events or play at concerts most Fridays and Saturdays, usually with a few of my kids in tow. To many, my job in itself seems a bit abnormal, especially when you add in our family situation and the way we go about life.

So far I have only described the outward things, which are visible. However, if I told you about all my personal oddities this early in the book, you would probably close it immediately! The point is, there is very little about my life that would be considered normal, even by my own definition.

Surprisingly, I can say this without shame or regret. I gave up my pursuit of normal a long time ago. To begin with, I was terrible at it! It is difficult for me to put my finger on when and where, but somewhere along the way I realized the normal I sought was a vapor. Whenever it appeared within reach, I was unable to grasp it. Have you ever tried to grab your breath on a cold morning? This was my dilemma. I soon realized that if I did in fact achieve some state of "normal," I might actually be bending down low, settling for something less.

But what if God had designed me not to bend down but to stretch up and reach for the stars? Not that normal is bad, but why should you or I settle for normal when we've been created for something far greater?

Normal. It's a fairly subjective word, yet we all seem to understand what it means. Encyclopedia.com defines it as "conforming to a standard; usual, typical, or expected."[1] This gives me mixed feelings. Sure, everyone likes to have some guidelines or, at the very least, a general road map to follow in their lives. We were all built with an innate desire to have our feet planted on something solid rather than having our lives suspended in midair.

Normal appears to offer this. Normal promises to be our steady. This brings us comfort and keeps us on task. Pursuing normal gives us a sense that we are in control as we set a standard upon which to base our expectations.

At the same time, normal shows us that we are not in control. When we were kids, normal was the home we wished we were born into, the color we wished our skin had been, or the texture we wanted our hair to have so we would fit in at school. Normal was the job we envisioned having, which hopefully came with health insurance and a 401(k). Normal was the natural cycle of life and death we expected to see in our families, with grandparents passing on peacefully at ripe old ages rather than children being pulled from our hands way too soon.

So how can normal be both our standard *and* our unattainable?

I wrote this book because my life testifies to this contradiction. As anyone who knows me can attest, my life has been anything but dictionary-definition normal. My childhood was pretty ordinary; I

We were all built with an innate desire to have our feet planted on something solid rather than having our lives suspended in midair.

was raised in a small town in South Carolina by two loving parents and with two siblings who fought an ordinary amount for siblings. After graduating from college, I got engaged to my high school sweetheart, Martin, and we enjoyed a fairly normal engagement and first year of marriage. Yet as we began that second year, Martin began to struggle with some issues with his memory and energy level.

Initially, it was hard to be sure something was wrong. What husband doesn't sometimes fall asleep while watching football or forget to mow the lawn? But when Martin fell asleep at the wheel on the interstate, we sought answers. Ultimately, Martin was diagnosed with a brain tumor.

This was decidedly not normal. And it was shocking news for this couple of newlyweds. The bright future we had envisioned now held a substantial roadblock. As Christ followers, we placed our full trust in God to help us through it. Knowing God could heal or fix anything, we fully anticipated seeing him work in tremendous and surprising ways through our trial. Looking back now, I see our faith wasn't misplaced. But we were a bit naïve. God did in fact accomplish tremendous and surprising things through Martin's brain tumor. He still does. But the scope of his work has proved vaster than anything we anticipated. Our greatest surprise has been in seeing how God chooses to bring himself immeasurable glory through what he has *not* healed and what he has *not* fixed.

After his surgery, Martin spent three months in the hospital, which was about two and a half months longer than expected. His tumor had been deeper and larger than estimated, the surgery had been more traumatic than anticipated, and he suffered complications that left us wondering from day to day whether he would, in fact, pull through. Yet as those long ICU days passed, we began to see small improvements, like the removal of tubes and the slow returning of speech and other mental faculties.

If you were to meet Martin today, it's possible you would have no idea he has a brain injury. He is the most charming, inquisitive, and jovial person you will ever meet. Just don't be surprised if he has to ask your name a few times. He lives with a short-term memory deficit as well as a substantial vision deficit. These disabilities have made it difficult for him to find work, and due to his vision loss, he is unable to drive. Still, his cognitive and reasoning abilities are untouched. He is an exceptionally bright guy. But his inability to see well or remember the smallest of details makes his life, and our family's, anything but normal.

My story may look different from yours, but each of us has something in our lives that has forced us to let go of whatever normalcy we envisioned. Maybe you are single and longing to be married, or you find yourself single *again*, carrying the forever ache of a promise not kept. Maybe you have had to embrace a different vocation from the one you had trained for, or you've been passed over for a promotion you had rightfully earned. Maybe an aging parent or the loss of a job is causing you to relocate, to move from the home and community where you have put down roots. Any number of things could be causing a departure from normal.

Or maybe normal isn't something you are leaving but something you never feel you had. Due to a shameful past, caused by your mistakes or maybe someone else's, normal has been something you have never experienced or could never quite attain. Where normal signifies wholeness, all you've ever known are brokenness, shame, and regret. Now you are just barely hanging on, wondering if anyone even notices. I don't know your story, but I can say that I've never met anyone who has said their life turned out exactly as planned. Every one of us has endured uninvited change. Every one of us will again be forced to wave goodbye to normal.

When Normal Says So Long to Us

Together with our neighbors, together with our country, and, in fact, together with the world, we entered 2020. Who could have known the year would go down in history as the most abnormal of our lifetimes? Not in our wildest dreams would we have imagined beginning the year with news of a dangerous virus with potential to spread beyond the single country where it originated. At first, we began thinking through how to ratchet up our household precautions against germs. Within weeks, government buildings worldwide were shutting down, countries were closing, schools were transitioning to remote learning, and businesses were shuttering—some to never reopen. And that describes only what happened logistically.

A good friend of mine is a chaplain in the Dallas area. Having extensively studied trauma, he defines it as "any situation or event that adversely disrupts the normal routine of someone's life."[2] If you agree with this definition, we must conclude that in 2020 we all endured trauma. Not one of us escaped having our normal affected by the global pandemic of COVID-19.

To truly process our collective trauma, we must begin by acknowledging the dramatic transformation of our homes—yes, those four walls in which you spent more time in 2020 than you ever imagined you would. I absolutely love my family, but I remember moments in those first few months when I would pretend I left something in my car just so I could go sit in it and have ten minutes alone without the incessant soundtrack of "Mommy! Mommy! Mommy!" I probably shouldn't admit that, but I also know I'm probably not alone. (You know who you are!)

For most of us, the home suddenly became the epicenter for all of life. This had its pros and cons. Families gathered around the dinner table, some for the first time and some for the first time in a long while. Working moms like me relearned to cook. We watched a lot of Netflix and Disney+, which I'll place in both the positive and negative categories. The pace of life we kept before was no longer an option, so we all slowed down. I've heard many people say that quarantine life provided them with a stillness they knew they needed but hadn't been able to achieve before.

While we've seen positive aspects of this pandemic, we're also aware of many negatives. People returning home to empty tables. Sitting alone, surrounded by a solitude that feels like dense fog. Desperately desiring the company of a friend or family member. Unable to overcome loneliness through the illusion of gathering with others through social media.

As the pandemic marched on with no abatement, many folks hit such a financial slump that their tables, once full, were now bare. And then there was the global impact of the pandemic measured in lives lost or health impacted. COVID-19 hasn't been a slight departure from our normal. It has turned everything upside down.

Gee, thanks, Laura, you might be thinking. *You don't need to remind me of everything that changed and everything that has been lost.*

I know it's hard, but please hang with me for a moment. It's important to honestly assess our losses and grieve them properly. But there is also a picture developing of what God is doing in and through our collective suffering. We need to see this every bit as clearly as we have witnessed the damage.

The tragic global and personal effects of the virus are not an ending to a final chapter. Our story is still being written. The daily changes and challenges that come our way feel new and often confuse or frustrate us. In reality, though it may be hard to understand or even believe, this present affliction is simply one chapter of a greater story—one that has been unfolding from the beginning of time. And it's certainly neither new nor surprising to the Author.

If, by the time you read this, you're living on the other side of those pandemic days, I'm sure something else is now at work causing strain and upheaval in your life. COVID-19 wasn't your first disruption of normal, and it won't be your last.

Sometimes normal simply says goodbye to *us*.

Reflecting on changes that result in the disappearance of normal is useful. When we are rocked back on our heels, when we find ourselves disoriented, we're forced to reconsider how desperately we've been holding on to things that we thought of as normal. If we are honest we know that it's during these times of uninvited disturbance that we are able to assign proper value to things lost. As the saying goes, we don't know what we have until it is gone. This has never been so evident as it is today.

Going through this strange season, I have been forced to consider how the so-called normal things of life have such a profound grip on me. When I think of the high schoolers I know who missed out on the milestones they've long anticipated—their senior proms, their baseball seasons, and even their graduation ceremonies—I grieve their memories, forever lost. One occurance I realized I had long taken for granted was a simple hug or handshake at church. Because I'm a worship leader, one of my favorite parts about Sunday was coming off the platform after the service and hugging the necks of friends and meeting visitors I didn't recognize. But social distancing, by definition, doesn't lend itself to affection. And it became increasingly harder to say to fellow church members, "I am with you" when I couldn't actually be with them. It felt a little funny to say to visitors, "Our church is so warm and inviting! Just don't get closer than six feet from me, and I probably won't even recognize you next week, since we're both wearing masks!"

But the losses are even weightier. I've heard of folks who had recently risked their life savings, along with borrowed money, on a dream of having their own restaurant or boutique, only to be shut down within a few weeks of opening. Dreams snuffed out before they ever had a chance.

And of course, countless families had to say goodbye to loved ones over the phone or Zoom, unable to sit at their bedsides holding their hands as they passed into glory.

Even as I recount these instances, I'm thinking of dozens of other stories. I'm sure you are too. Perhaps even your own.

A Greater Story

What could possibly compensate for such painful losses? As a Christian I truly draw comfort from the Word of God, but quoting a Bible verse in the midst of such grief feels like a spiritual Band-Aid. The truth is we don't always have satisfying responses for such questions. But if we can believe that God is writing a greater story, we may be able to move ahead without definitive answers.

If we can believe that God is writing a greater story, we may be able to move ahead without definitive answers.

So let me ask a different question: Is it possible God is working in and through these circumstances in ways we can't imagine this side of heaven? And is it possible the work he is doing begins with us saying goodbye to normal?

That day on the zip-line platform, I was forced to wave adios to my normal, my steady, my comfort. And the next thing I knew, I was soaring.

I was also screaming and flailing and feeling my breakfast come up a bit. But I was soaring. My coworkers looked like little ants below me, cheering me on (or maybe just laughing at me). Sometime between leaving that wooden platform and whizzing past the blur of trees and church buildings, I realized something: what felt like a free fall wasn't that at all. I never ceased being safely tethered to something sturdy and sure.

I'm not here to sugarcoat the brokenness we see around us. I promise you my goal in writing this book is more than merely encouraging an attitude shift toward positivity. My hope for you and me is that whenever we face the loss of normal, we encounter God, seeing with fresh eyes the work he might be doing there. It's why I've included five unique stories from other families and friends in our church, people who have faced their own unique challenges with normal and seen God use those challenges to grow them in ways they weren't expecting. If you are willing to go with me on this journey, all I ask is that you keep an open mind, open heart, and open hands. Maybe you need a nudge, like I did with the zip line. Consider this book your nudge, because little by little we can learn to say so long to normal.

I can assure you that the benefits will outweigh the perceived losses. As we begin, we must be willing to discipline our minds to process information and events in a manner that may be counter-cultural. In this journey, we will travel through our hearts as we grieve the heaviness of life and the loss of relationships. Yet "hope springs eternal in the human breast."[3] Our hearts will be renewed with hopefulness. Finally, we'll be able to open our hands and let go of things, people, and paradigms we once leaned on that, as it turned out, weren't sturdy enough to support us forever.

As you wave goodbye to these things, the future may not be as clear as you desire, but you will face it with fresh spiritual eyes. You'll see something that is greater by far than the normal you've held so tightly. Slowly but surely your mind will align with the mind of Christ and his Word. Your heart will find joy in the someone who is sturdier than your circumstances.

You may feel frightened, as any person in their right mind should as they step away from a seemingly secure foundation. Your surroundings might get a little blurry as you wait for the rope to snatch you, saving you from the expectation of certain death. And when it does, you'll experience a jolt that will take your breath away.

But here's what I can assure you: the rope will hold. You may flail and flounder, but the rope will hold. You will be held by a foundation of promises, pledged to you by the one who gave his very Son that you might know his love, his peace, and his provision. And the hands of the one who holds us are sturdier than any old normal we once held on to with a death grip. He is our sure and steady hope that guides us to embrace the beautiful story unfolding before our very eyes.

The invitation is simple. Join me on this exhilarating adventure of saying goodbye to normal and hello to unshakable faith!

Part One

Understanding Normal

He has made everything beautiful in its time.
Also, he has put eternity into man's heart,
yet so that he cannot find out what God has
done from the beginning to the end.

—ECCLESIASTES 3:11

Chapter One

Why We Crave Normal

Every morning right at 6:00 a.m. the glorious sound of percolating begins. I head downstairs to my seat. And when I say "my seat" I mean the spot on the couch I guard passionately. It features a small lamp, my Bible, a notebook, a few books, and a little spot for my coffee cup. It's my seat.

Actually my morning routine begins even before I get up. The previous night, I meticulously prepare my trusty coffee maker and check the timer twice to make sure it's fully equipped to do its job the next morning. I like to get a jump on the day. Every now and then, if I've been out late at an event, I'll sleep in until eight o'clock or so. But let's face it, sleeping in and having young children are not exceedingly compatible.

Martin and the kids know there is nothing that will get them a cold bowl of cereal for breakfast quicker than sitting in my seat. My husband thinks it's completely irrational that someone else sitting in my seat has the ability to completely turn my day upside down. But, strangely, somehow it does. I like my seat! I like my routine! Step off, family, and give me this one thing in life!

The truth is, I don't fully understand why my routine is so important to me, but most people I talk to share the same affection for theirs. What's your morning ritual? Maybe you're an early riser, or maybe you're a more nocturnal soul who loves to sleep in. Your morning routine might include a favorite coffee shop where the owner greets you by name and has your order started before you reach the register. Maybe it's going for a run at daybreak or an early workout. Or perhaps it's simply checking your news app of choice to see what events happened the day before.

Something in us likes to create patterns in our days and stick to them. Don't get me wrong; I love an adventure. Many of our family outings are spent hiking, barreling into the unknown with a can of bug spray and some Betty Crocker Fruit Roll-Ups. But when the adventure is over, it's nice to return to the familiarity of home, the predictable rhythm of a schedule—not to mention the convenience of an indoor toilet. What is it about normal that feels so safe and comforting?

The deeper we dig into this question, the closer we'll come to identifying a key reality about ourselves as humans. Our yearning for rituals, routines, and established patterns is not a new concept. But why do we crave them so?

First, let me ask you this: How do you think this yearning found its way into the fabric of who we are as humans? We can gain some insight into this from the book of Ecclesiastes. This is a book of the Bible that most of us either love or love to skip over. I have often thought that if Solomon, widely considered the author of Ecclesiastes, were writing it today, his publisher would have warned against making "Vanity of vanities! All is vanity" his opening line (Eccl. 1:2). Yet by the third chapter, Solomon brings everything into balance.

"He [God] has made everything appropriate [some translations say *beautiful*] in its time," it reads. "*He has also set eternity in their heart"* (Eccl. 3:11 NASB, emphasis added). This can be a difficult verse to understand. In one sense, this setting of eternity in the heart represents the image of God that is in all humans, his *imago Dei.*

In Genesis 1:27, we read that "God created man in his own image." If this is our starting point, we can surely understand our restlessness, our yearning to know this God in whose image we've been created. There is a longing deeply settled in the souls of mankind that wants to touch the infinite, to share in the Immortal's eternal existence. Saint Augustine (AD 354–430) summarized it this way: "You have made us for Your sake, and our hearts are restless until they rest in You."[1]

Much further down the road, Canadian missionary Don Richardson discovered that this idea of eternity in our hearts was understood even in the most primitive of cultures, which made it an effective way of communicating the gospel despite cultural barriers. Though the tribal people he served in New Guinea had never before heard the name of Jesus, they somehow knew their hearts held a unique need that they alone were unable to fill.[2]

Let's go back to our vanity-of-vanities book for a second. Chapter 3 of Ecclesiastes may contain the answer to our question of why normal feels so safe and comforting. It also seems to answer the question of why we crave it. Read with me:

For everything there is a season, and a time for every matter under heaven:

> a time to be born, and a time to die;
> a time to plant, and a time to pluck up what is planted;
> a time to kill, and a time to heal;
> a time to break down, and a time to build up;

a time to weep, and a time to laugh;

a time to mourn, and a time to dance;

a time to cast away stones, and a time to gather stones together;

a time to embrace, and a time to refrain from embracing;

a time to seek, and a time to lose;

a time to keep, and a time to cast away;

a time to tear, and a time to sew;

a time to keep silence, and a time to speak;

a time to love, and a time to hate;

a time for war, and a time for peace. (vv. 1–8)

I've heard this passage read aloud at funerals of both Christians and non-Christians. There is something deeply comforting about the orderliness of life. It soothes us to know that there is an appointed time for every thing and every event this side of heaven, even death. Solomon in his wisdom wasn't coming from a fatalistic mindset, implying that we are all simply victims of cosmic forces beyond our control. He was writing to console and reassure us.

Look again at the list above. Notice the balance of truths. Life contains hard things we must deal with. But those things are counterbalanced with positive and even desirable outcomes. Is there death and dying in this world? Yes. But there is also a time for birth. Will there be wars and strife? Sadly, yes. But there *will* also be a time for peace.

Here's one I find particularly compelling, having experienced such a long season of social distancing during the COVID-19 pandemic: Are there times to embrace? Yes. As we've learned, there are also times to refrain from embracing.

Do you see how each of these simple yet profound back-and-forth statements points to the many facets of our lives? These patterns repeat over and over from one generation to another, and they hold true for everyone, everywhere. This is the universal experience of all humans. As we set out together, this broader understanding of life's natural rhythms helps us understand why we're attracted to familiar patterns.

Just like I'm attracted to my morning routine. (Keep out of my seat!)

Back to the Garden

Although it precedes my era in the music industry, I think of a line in a Crosby, Stills, Nash & Young rock song from long ago: "We've got to get ourselves back to the garden."[3] When I sing lyrics like this, I resonate with the yearning it expresses. Whether we discern it or not, it sits at or below the surface of who we are and how we interact with others. We all long for security, stability, and firm footing. We all long to get ourselves back to the garden.

But what could this yearning possibly have to do with the garden? And do we agree with Crosby, Stills, Nash & Young that we're trying to get back there?

Consider the wonders of the creation of the world and the garden of Eden. To understand this normal we crave, let's go back to the very beginning.

We all long for security, stability, and firm footing. We all long to get ourselves back to the garden.

In the beginning, God created the heavens and the earth. The earth was without form and void, and darkness was over the face of the deep. And the Spirit of God was hovering over the face of the waters.

And God said, "Let there be light," and

there was light. And God saw that the light was good. And God separated the light from the darkness. God called the light Day, and the darkness he called Night. And there was evening and there was morning, the first day. (Gen. 1:1–5)

God was creating cosmic order! He spoke, and that which had never existed now came into existence. Thomas Edison invented the light bulb, but God made light itself! Can you even imagine such a scene? And he didn't stop there.

And God said, "Let there be an expanse in the midst of the waters, and let it separate the waters from the waters." And God made the expanse and separated the waters that were under the expanse from the waters that were above the expanse. And it was so. And God called the expanse Heaven. And there was evening and there was morning, the second day. (vv. 6–8)

God continued to create something out of nothing on days three, four, and five. For the sake of time, let's skip forward to his tremendous work on days six and seven.

And God said, "Let the earth bring forth living creatures according to their kinds—livestock and creeping things and beasts of the earth according to their kinds." And it was so. And God made the beasts of the earth according to their kinds and the livestock according to their kinds, and everything that creeps on the ground according to its kind. And God saw that it was good.

Then God said, "Let us make man in our image, after our likeness. And let them have dominion over the fish of the sea and over the birds of the heavens and over the livestock and over all the earth and over every creeping thing that creeps on the earth."

> So God created man in his own image,
> in the image of God he created him;
> male and female he created them. (vv. 24–27)

This, in a nutshell, is the story of the creation of the world. Out of the chaos, God brought order. And once the land, sea, and animals were in place, he created man. The description of God's next actions are also captured in Genesis. "The LORD God planted a garden toward the east, in Eden; and there He placed the man whom He had formed" (Gen. 2:8 NASB). This was an anticipatory move on God's part, given his divine omniscience. He knew what man would need before man became aware of his own needs.

The garden wasn't only meant to supply man's need for a bounty of fruit and vegetables. You see, God placed man in the garden of Eden to cultivate and keep it, to give him meaningful and purposeful work. And God also knew that more would be needed. He hadn't designed man to flourish from work alone. Nor had he designed him as a solitary being. So once again God did what he always does: he provided what was necessary before man even recognized his lack. At this point in the narrative, Eve joined Adam. Now, not only did Adam have meaningful work but, with Eve as his companion, he no longer labored alone.

Think for a moment of your own job. Ever struggled with budget cuts? Long work hours? Sudden layoffs? Constant pressure from leadership to please shareholders? Scrap all those ideas when it comes to Eden. Together Adam and Eve worked the garden, and their labor was not toilsome. Their daily work was not unwelcome, and they didn't resent its place in their lives. It was simply a part of the natural rhythm of life that had been ordained by God the Father.

Work was joyful. It was life-giving rather than life-draining. This work was held in proper balance along with the other facets of their lives. Remember that during the creation process we saw God himself model a rhythm of work and rest.

So often, we see work as a necessary evil, something to avoid. This was not Adam and Eve's experience. Work was received as a blessing from God.

Life for Adam and Eve was something we can only imagine or dream of experiencing. They lived together in perfect harmony with each other. There were no marital disputes. No tiffs over socks left on the floor or squabbles over who unloaded the dishwasher last. Not only was there no external conflict; there was no internal conflict. No anxiety. No depression. No need that went unsatisfied. Just beauty. Safety. Peace.

The first couple routinely fellowshipped with God the Father in the cool of the day. I imagine them sitting comfortably with their creator, asking questions similar to the kinds my own children ask me—youthful and innocent. No embarrassment, no fear of looking stupid, and certainly no impatience on the Father's part. Are you beginning to see what made Eden so amazing?

Reading the account in Genesis, we can glean insight into the rituals that were Adam and Eve's "normal." Of course, there is much we can't know. Filmmakers have tried to portray life in the garden. Writers have attempted epic poems and novels about it.

Sit back for a moment and let your mind imagine anything that would make your life wonderful. A cruise to the Caribbean? A day at the spa? Or how about just one conflict-free family gathering? I believe that whatever comes to your mind won't begin to compare with the daily experience of Adam and Eve. It was, after all, the garden of Eden.

Living East of Eden

What changed? And how did this change so distort normal that no one's been able to re-create it this side of heaven? We know the change involved a serpent and some fruit. But more than that, it started with the question, "Did God really say . . . ?"

A simple question with incredible implications. This question set Adam and Eve on a path that forever changed their relationship with God, their relationship with each other, and their relationship with their environment. When human sin entered the garden, it brought with it changes of cosmic proportions. Changes that would reach through generations and across all cultures. To this day, we still suffer the consequences of this question and Eve's response.

> Now the serpent was more crafty than any of the wild animals the LORD God had made. He said to the woman, "Did God really say, 'You must not eat from any tree in the garden'?"
>
> The woman said to the serpent, "We may eat fruit from the trees in the garden, but God did say, 'You must not eat fruit from the tree that is in the middle of the garden, and you must not touch it, or you will die.'"
>
> "You will not certainly die," the serpent said to the woman. "For God knows that when you eat from it your eyes will be opened, and you will be like God, knowing good and evil." (Gen. 3:1–5 NIV)

How interesting that Adam and Eve were so content, and yet somehow the serpent was able to suggest there was something better! He planted a thought: *God is holding out on you.* In effect, this was really an attack on the most fundamental question: *Can God be trusted?* Despite all their pleasures, Adam and Eve began to doubt.

After reading this story over and over, I've come to a mini-revelation. Adam and Eve were living life to the fullest. Theirs was a life of harmony, peace, and fulfillment. And as I look back over my own life, I'm amazed that I, too, have enjoyed seasons when life was filled with ease and prosperity, relatively free of hardships. My experience during these good and easy times has been that I've dropped my guard a little—just enough to begin living life in my own strength, moving through my days and weeks with little consultation with God. So what's my revelation? It's been during those times of relative ease that I've been most susceptible to the whispered question of the serpent, "Indeed, has God said?" which in turn has led to doubts about what I've been called to do or, in some cases, not do.

Like many of you, I'm also driven to doubt when under severe stress, dealing with hurt and pain, or facing unknowns. But for some reason, during those harder times, I'm more likely to run to the Father. It's when I have no hurdles or resistance that I begin to function on autopilot. Perhaps I've been fooled into thinking I can expect to live in garden-of-Eden-style normal. I've forgotten: that ideal of normal ended long ago.

Can you relate?

Isn't it fascinating to consider how everything in creation and in our own lives was turned upside down because of Adam's and Eve's sin? And yet, even through the disappointment of the first couple's fall from grace, we see the kindness and faithfulness of God. After Adam and Eve were deceived and ate of the forbidden fruit, the story

> Perhaps I've been fooled into thinking I can expect to live in garden-of-Eden-style normal. I've forgotten: that ideal of normal ended long ago.

continued. "They heard the sound of the LORD God walking in the garden in the cool of the day, and the man and his wife hid themselves from the presence of the LORD God among the trees of the garden" (Gen. 3:8–9 NASB).

The God who created everything and knows everything bent low toward Adam and Eve and played along with their childish game of hide-and-seek. "Where are you?" he asked (v. 9 NASB). His question was amazing and far more profound than the question asked by the serpent. Whereas the serpent's question resulted in destruction, God's question resulted in restoration. God knew exactly where Adam and Eve were—not just physically but spiritually and emotionally. He was God! No, this question was for the benefit of Adam and Eve. God was helping them become self-aware. In a sense, the serpent's promise was indeed coming to pass.

They would know things they had never known before. And yet, even through the disappointment of the first couple's fall from grace (Gen. 3:22–24), we see the kindness and faithfulness of God.

As God lovingly pursued their hearts and walked them through a very deliberate process of confession, forgiveness, and reconciliation, he set eternity in their hearts on another level. He offered them a promise, the same promise he offers us today. A promise of future deliverance, a promise of one day returning things to a God-designed normal.

However, until the day Jesus returns, their journey—and ours—will be filled with peril and challenges as well as moments of joy and thanksgiving. Hearts will be shaken. Lives will be rocked. Yet God will remain steadfast.

Does this help explain why we crave normal? Does it make your heart ache for what was lost and long for what is to come? My hope is not to leave us in a depressing place, or leave us mad at Adam and Eve for blowing it for all of us. My point is this: we were designed by an orderly God to thrive in an orderly world. But just like Adam and Eve, we have no choice but to say so long to the garden and step into the world that lies east of Eden. Until Jesus returns, and the garden is restored, we'll continue to crave a sense of order and normalcy that will always be beyond our reach. The first step is this acknowledgment about ourselves. The next step is seeing how this affects our day-to-day lives and our world.

Chapter Two

The Shaking of What
Can Be Shaken

Have you ever chosen a word of the year? Until a few years ago, I didn't realize this was even a thing. Several of the women in my small group mentioned they had benefited from selecting a single word, maybe an attribute of God or a biblical truth, to focus on throughout the year. So in January 2020, I decided to try it and chose the word *steadfast*. I had just finished a Bible study by that title,[1] and with all the craziness of my life, it seemed like a great choice for my word of the year. One of my friends even made me a key necklace with the word *steadfast* engraved on it. What could possibly go wrong?

As a matter of fact, 2020 did start off pretty normal. We had our whole year planned out, with concerts and speaking events almost every weekend, including a couple of international trips. Our daughter, Josie, was rocking first grade, things at the church where I work were plugging along, and our family dynamics were fairly stable.

But that all changed the second week of March.

"Have you heard anything about this new coronavirus?" a co-worker asked. "They're thinking we may even have to cancel church this weekend." Cancel church? In the forty-three-year history of Perimeter Church, never had Sunday service been canceled. Even that time we had a tornado literally rip through our campus on the morning of Good Friday, knocking out the electricity, we *still* held a service at noon!

Little did we know, the following weeks and months would be spent taping a series of services to stream online over the coming Sundays. Our building would close and remain that way for months to come. And in addition to the drastic changes at work, things were quickly changing at home. We made bizarre grocery-store runs, fully masked and gloved. Early on, I felt fearful showing up to empty store shelves, not sure what I would feed the kids. Another level of fear arrived when the toilet-paper section stayed bare for weeks. I won't even tell you how creative our family became in that area!

And then followed the joyous experience we came to know as remote learning. I became teacher, headmaster, guidance counselor, and lunch lady in one fell swoop. Yes, I had some sweet moments with Josie, like when she was learning how to do fractions for the first time. But she and I both recognized early on that I should have been paying better attention in elementary school myself. I like to joke about the predicament we found ourselves in, but I don't mean to make light of it.

In the weeks that followed, we would hear many stories much harder than our own. We saw the headlines of lives lost, jobs ended, and continuous political fallout. As families went into quarantine, grandparents could no longer visit their grandkids. Friends were relegated to hanging out on Zoom. Businesses shut down, workers were laid off, and live events were canceled.

And personally, when I say live events were canceled, I don't mean a few dates on a calendar. I mean twenty-five to thirty speaking and singing engagements I had planned and prayed for, and concerts and retreats for which tickets had been sold. I'm speaking of events that planning committees had worked on tirelessly, investing both time and money. The mass of cancellations was jarring to say the least, especially as I reflected on my use of album sales to purchase diapers for my two-year-old!

Steadfast? I kept asking God. *Is that really my word for this year?*

As if the widespread instability of a global pandemic wasn't enough, another incident knocked me to the ground. And I mean literally knocked me to the ground. Three weeks into our state's mandated lockdown, I headed out for a bike ride. With everything from coffee shops to state parks closed, riding was one of the only ways I could still find a bit of me time. As I was pulling out of the driveway, while adjusting my shoelaces and taking a call for work (yeah, really dumb, I know), my tire hit a small patch of leaves I hadn't seen. Within half a second, *wham!* I hit the pavement hard enough to fracture my right elbow, and I badly scraped my arm and leg as I slid. Long story short, I ended up in the emergency room watching a very nice nurse pick gravel out of my flesh with tweezers. I departed with a cast that went from my armpit to my elbow.

The following two weeks were some of the most difficult I had faced in a long while. While trying to homeschool Josie, balance work-related Zoom calls, and manage the cancellation and rescheduling of our entire spring tour, I was operating with only one working arm. One arm to change the baby's diaper. One arm to chop potatoes for dinner. I couldn't drive, or ride my bike, or do a thousand other things I had taken for granted.

Blessedly, the whole family was eager to help Mommy. The kids helped with meal prep. Martin, a diaper-changing champ, picked up any slack with Baby Timothy. Josie stuck close by my side, helping me get dressed, tying my shoes, even fixing my hair. I had become her life-size American Girl doll. I wish I had thought to take some screenshots of my extravagant hairdos for all those Zoom calls! Griffin became my little encourager, bringing me flowers and pictures he had drawn. Benji and Timothy, on the other hand, did not like the new one-armed Mommy. Tim just stared at the long cast on my arm that made it impossible for me to pick him up, screamed at me, and ran off. Benji, feeling the same way yet more verbally articulate, announced each morning, "I'm gonna go hug Dad instead. I like hugging people with two arms!"

I can now look back and laugh, but I also recognize the deep work God was doing in my heart. If there are two aspects of my personality in which I often place too much trust, it's my planning and my abilities. I like to have a plan, preferably one that covers twelve or even eighteen months in advance. With a good, thorough plan, I feel pretty confident in my ability to carry things out. We schedule the events and book the flights, then go do them. If it's on the calendar, it's as good as done.

But in 2020, it was as if someone took a big eraser to my well-planned life. Every meticulously detailed preparation suddenly vanished. The personal strengths I had once leaned on to do what needed to be done in any given moment appeared worthless.

And my word of the year? I needed steadfastness more than I could have ever dreamed. With everything constantly changing, I needed to trust God to be our steady, our rock, and our firm foundation. My word of the year became a running joke around our house. We even decided to hang the key necklace my friend had made on a small nail by the refrigerator. Whenever I became overwhelmed and appeared about to blow, Griffin would whisper to the other kids, "Quick! Mom needs her key!"

The More Things Change

Whether your situation looked similar to mine or not, every one of us has experienced something in life that has shaken us.

Change comes in many shapes and through many different circumstances. The changes that shake us can be serious, such as the loss of a job or the death of a loved one. Or they can be positive, natural progressions of life, like a child graduating high school and leaving home to start college or a job promotion that requires a change in the family's daily routine and maybe even a geographic change. Anyone who has ever taken that exciting journey of fostering or adopting a child knows that even the clearest calling to take such a step doesn't ensure an easy road.

Disruption of our normal can arrive slowly over time, or it can happen overnight.

Life is like a familiar, well-worn path. As you walk along, sometimes for years, you give little thought to the path until, seemingly all of a sudden and without the courtesy of forewarning, the path beneath your feet that once seemed so solid, so sure, begins to shift. At first it may be hardly discernible. This is a favorite ploy of sci-fi films. The filmmaker manipulates the audience at a subliminal level by showing just enough to create anxiety. The audience senses impending doom, though they may not know why. They desperately want to call out to the character, "Watch out! Things are not what they seem to be!"

As we discovered in the previous chapter, things are *not* what they once were. We live east of Eden. Ever since the fall of humanity in chapter 3 of Genesis, normal has been distorted. We reach for anything solid to stabilize us along the path, but most of those things we thought were sturdy eventually give way.

Change is a wild card, introducing an element of uncertainty. Change feels shaky. No wonder we resist it.

Any life change causes stress. In the business world, there are entire areas of study on the topic of *change management*. I heard once that when organizations are super-resistant to change, they engage in "guerrilla warfare." Remember those big monkeys battling in a postapocalyptic world in the old classic movie *Planet of the Apes*? Not that kind of gorilla—but that's what I pictured when I first heard this. When I snapped back into the conversation, I learned that because change is so stressful, personnel will work to appear on the surface as if they're on board with changes while in fact they're plotting undercover to keep everything exactly as it is.

We can try to fight it, but to live is to change. Yes, change is often hard, but change is inevitable. If we're no longer experiencing any changes in our lives, there is a good chance that our body temperatures have settled to room temperature. So, with this as our reality, here is the question: *How do we become the kind of disciples who embrace change?*

Becoming Unshakable

Here is the good news not only of this chapter but of the book as a whole: when life becomes shaky, we do not have to be shaken.

As my key necklace often reminds me, we can remain steadfast. How can I say this with such confidence? Because this is what the Scriptures teach. The Bible speaks clearly about a type of shaking that our loving God allows. This shaking is not random. This shaking is not unsupervised. This shaking is not without some purpose that will benefit us.

When life becomes shaky, we do not have to be shaken.

Throughout the entire Bible, Scripture tells us not to be fearful or discouraged when we are in the midst of this God-allowed shaking. Why? Because it's a means to an end. God is leveraging our circumstances to make us sturdier and more stable. He wants us to have an unshakable faith.

But in the Christian's experience, this does not happen overnight.

Let me illustrate this point with something my kids and I observed in our neighborhood. On our bike-riding days, we often passed a vacant lot. One day the lot that had been vacant for so long was transformed. Bulldozers had been brought onto the property, and they had dug a deep pit. It looked like an army bunker. The kids were confused. They knew this was going to be a house, but nothing about it seemed to line up with their experience of houses.

I'm no architect or builder, so I can't tell you exactly what the builders were doing beyond creating a foundation, but I can testify that they did it for a long time. They measured the area, leveled the surface, and poured concrete, then repeated that process over and over. Every few days when we rode by, we saw little visible evidence of progress. Then one day they began to build the actual house. The floor was laid, the walls were erected, and in no time at all a house was standing on a piece of land that had formerly been a field. The kids were amazed. Heck, who am I kidding? I was amazed also.

The illustration is obvious. To build a dependable house, one must follow a process to lay a proper foundation. Engineering must take place. Codes must not be overlooked. The construction of the actual house would have been in vain if the foundation had been unstable.

I can't help but be reminded of the parable Jesus told about two builders. One built on shifting sand, and the other on a firm foundation. I suspect, on first glance, the house built on shifting sand didn't appear much different from the other house. But then "the rain fell and the floods came, and the winds blew and slammed against that house; and it fell—and its collapse was great" (Matt. 7:27 NASB). You could Joanna Gaines the inside of that house all day long, but without a stable foundation it wouldn't stand.

During the housing market crash of 2008, we purchased our home for about 60 percent of its value, which is why we could afford it. When we moved in, we knew there was much work to be done. One of its not-so-fabulous features was a back deck that was missing a few support beams underneath. "Don't even step on it," we were strongly warned.

I noticed it wasn't visibly sagging. "It can't be that bad," I said to Martin. "Do we really need to replace it? Can't we just throw some patio furniture on it and see what happens?" Martin has always been wiser and more cautious in these kinds of situations, and he made me promise I wouldn't risk it. And I'm so very glad he did. His caution no doubt saved us from serious injury—because even though it appeared sturdy, that deck was an accident waiting to happen.

On a spiritual level (pun intended), is it possible that God in his mercy might allow our lives to be shaken for the sole purpose of exposing a faulty foundation? If he is as rich in mercy and abounding in love as we believe him to be, wouldn't it be unkind for him to allow us to keep building our lives on faulty foundations that will ultimately give way? Is it possible that in *kindness* he allows trials, yearning for us to let go of the false building blocks of this world, training us to cling only to that which cannot be shaken? Let's dig deeper into this idea.

Where Hope Is Built

The writer of Hebrews quoted an Old Testament prophecy that spoke of a shaking that would happen to the people of God. "'Yet once more I will shake not only the earth but also the heavens.' This phrase, 'Yet once more,' indicates the removal of things that are shaken—that is, things that have been made—in order that the things that cannot be shaken may remain" (12:26–27). In the prophecy's original context, God wasn't just allowing the prophesied shaking; he was causing it.

That's a whole lot of shakin' going on! Let me try to simplify the core of this passage. Sometimes God, in his kindness and mercy, intentionally allows a shaking away of the shaky foundations in our lives. It's like panning for gold. Our family did this once when we traveled to Alaska for an event. Our kids stood in the rain wearing bright yellow ponchos, catching sandy mud in a pan, then shaking and sifting all the debris out until, ideally, all that would be left was gold. Josie, being the first to find a minuscule speck, exclaimed, "Is this really it? I thought it would be bigger!"

Let's get personal. If the gold in this illustration is Jesus and his rich promises and plans for us, what are the dross and debris? Ask yourself, *What do I fill my life with that I cherish as if it were gold?* As one of my favorite theologians, F. F. Bruce, said, these things might be good things! I am not suggesting we compare our spouses, children, parents, jobs, feelings, homes, or other hard-earned stuff to debris. Those could be wonderful desires. But the only way we will know for sure whether we are holding them in their rightful place is through the sifting process. It is ultimately for our benefit when God allows good things to be shaken from our grip! He's teaching us to stop looking to them, rather than him, for our identity, security, and satisfaction.

When we allow God to be our source for these things, everything else becomes a blessing rather than a necessity. We stop expecting perfection from our spouses. The performance reviews that used to sting us to the core can be sources of vocational betterment rather than indictments on who we are as people, because we know Jesus declares our value, not our supervisors. When our children misbehave, as children tend to do, we can forgive them and shepherd their hearts with grace and endurance, for our hearts are not anchored to their successes and failures. Instead, our hearts are anchored to the forever-faithfulness of a perfect God. As 1 Peter 4:19 reminds us, we can commit "the keeping of [our] souls" to our "faithful Creator" (KJV).

When God is our foundation, we can let everyone and everything else off the hook.

When God is our foundation, we can let everyone and everything else off the hook.

Consider Martin's motives in our real-life scenario with the precarious deck. Was he trying to put a damper on my fun? Absolutely not. He desired my safety. He would never let me place my trust in something he knew would collapse and hurt me in the long run. And it is infinitely truer that God's motives are good. He longs to see us thrive, to live abundant and full lives. He loves us too much to allow us to tether our hearts to weights that will ultimately sink us. He cares too much to leave us standing on shifting sand when he rescued us from the dominion of darkness to stand on the only sure foundation: himself.

Over time, I have realized that I spend an enormous amount of emotional and mental energy trying to feel stable and secure. If I can book a full slate of concerts each year, I feel secure financially. If Martin maintains his current regimen of medications and diligently meets with his team of skilled doctors, I feel secure in his continued good health. If my children bring home good grades and glowing progress reports, Martin and I feel more secure about their educational outcome. With a good education, they're more likely to find stable jobs—and eventually move out and do their own laundry! You see what I mean? Though these are certainly not bad aspirations, they're not foundations upon which to place my hope.

If I know rationally that the things of this earth will give way, and the eternal things, the promises of who God is and what he has done, are the only true sources of stability in life, why in the world do I keep trying to lean on that which I know intellectually will not hold me?

Why do we keep investing so heavily in foundations built on shifting sand?

You may have your own reasons, but here's mine: Worldly things I can control. God I cannot. Worldly things I can often predict, manage, regulate, and manipulate. God I cannot. Worldly things I can see (and often, with the right resources, acquire). God I cannot.

I feel as though I have laid my heart before you. I hope you will not think less of me. But let me make one final admission about control: I love it. I love determining outcomes and directing resources as I see fit. But I now understand that control is an illusion.

No one asked me if all this shaking in the year 2020 was okay! No one asked me how long it should last. No one asked what level of shaking I felt comfortable with. And frankly, for a person who wants to be in control, I've been a little miffed. But I'm learning that my foundation of control is weak and unstable. It's shifting sand.

There is one foundation, and only one, suitable for you and me to stand on—God himself. As Psalm 62 reminds us, God alone is our rock and salvation. And as David says, with confidence, "I shall not be greatly shaken" (v. 2). We will always find God unshakable, worthy of our trust.

How much easier faith would be if we could just sit down with Jesus over a cup of coffee! Some of you might think of him as a pour-over kind of guy, but I'm pretty sure he's just a regular old Folgers fan like me.

Anyway, I would sit with him in my morning spot and tell him what's been going on lately, about how hard it has been to potty train Timothy. I'd ask him how I might be a better mother to the older three. I'd ask how I could know which one is lying when I find a family heirloom broken and every single one of them says, "I didn't do it!" (Actually, I could just ask him which one did it. He is, after all, omniscient!)

And I would ask the hard questions. Should I expect my foundation to be shaken again anytime soon? Will Martin's health issues relapse? Will we get to grow old together, or will one of us pass on to glory sooner rather than later? And what was God thinking when he made me so quirky? I bet Jesus would listen to my incessant ramblings. He'd probably chuckle at how worked up I get about silly things. And he'd reach over and wipe away a tear when I shared my deepest insecurities and most vulnerable failures. Just being able to sit across from him would bring such comfort to my soul.

I bet you, too, could rattle off a list of questions you'd like to ask Jesus. One day this will be a reality. One day it will be our only reality. Can you imagine? What a sweet day that will be.

Staying Steadfast

Meanwhile, you and I already possess much of Jesus. What we have today must be today's foundation. We have assurance of our salvation, orchestrated by our heavenly Father, accomplished through Christ's finished work on the cross, and sealed by the Holy Spirit. We have a Comforter, sent by Jesus to shore up our failing hearts while we await his return. We have the gift of his Word, sweeter than honey on our lips—a lamp to wandering feet and a light to shadowy paths. His Word is rock-solid truth in a world of shifting sand.

It may sound trite, but this is what we must cling to: God is our foundation. And he is no wobbly deck. We can throw our full weight and our whole hope upon his promises, believing he is sturdy enough for whatever shaking we may endure. His steadfastness warrants ours.

Joni Eareckson Tada, one of my heroes, demonstrates this kind of faith better than anyone I know. As you may be aware, Joni, now in her early seventies, survived an unfortunate diving accident as a teenager that left her a quadriplegic. Despite her disability, she would tell you her life has been full. Through her thriving speaking ministry and the foundation she began more than forty years ago that comes alongside families dealing with disabilities, Joni has blessed literally millions of people.

A few years back I had the honor of joining Joni onstage as her accompanist. She was supposed to speak and I was supposed to sing. But the more she shared her story, the more she burst into song! Don't get me wrong; she was honest about how hard life is for her. But it was as if she was incapable of sharing her story without singing of God's faithfulness through the struggle. Everyone joined as we sang anthem after anthem about God's goodness, including a hymn from 1834, "The Solid Rock," until the event organizers finally kicked us off the stage! Joni's determination not to allow her trials to dampen her worship, but rather to deepen it, was contagious. You won't find her focusing on what she has lost but on the work God has done in her and through her, *through* all she has lost.

The words from that old hymn still ring true today.

> My hope is built on nothing less
> Than Jesus' blood and righteousness;
> I dare not trust the sweetest frame,
> But wholly lean on Jesus' name.

On Christ, the solid Rock, I stand—
All other ground is sinking sand,
All other ground is sinking sand.

When darkness veils His lovely face,
I rest on His unchanging grace;
In ev'ry high and stormy gale
My anchor holds within the veil.

His oath, His covenant, His blood
Support me in the o'erwhelming floods;
When all around my soul gives way,
He then is all my hope and stay.

On Christ, the solid Rock, I stand—
All other ground is sinking sand,
All other ground is sinking sand.[2]

Remember, Christ never said we must have big faith to not be shaken. On the contrary, all that's needed is faith the size of a mustard seed in our big God (Matt. 17:20). It is not the greatness of our faith that upholds us. It is the greatness of our God.

Let me ask you this: What "normal" thing in your life do you think God could be sovereignly shaking to reveal to you something that is sturdier, truer, and ultimately unshakable?

Pray for courage to embrace change, knowing that when our world is shaken, we will always discover an unwavering God in the center of what may at first appear to be chaos. We can learn to say so long to all that God lovingly shakes from our lives, another step on our journey of saying so long to normal.

Part Two

Saying So Long

Jesus told his disciples, "If anyone would come after me, let him deny himself and take up his cross and follow me."

—MATTHEW 16:24

Chapter Three

So Long, Home

I had never attended a single service at Perimeter Church, located outside Atlanta, Georgia, until my first week on staff. Martin and I had spent the first year of our marriage in Spartanburg, South Carolina, serving with a local college ministry. It was an incredible way to start out together, pouring into a group of singles who were just a few years behind us, helping them navigate life and faith. But we'd also been feeling called somewhere else. It began as a small itch in Martin to study graphic design, which led us to a fabulous school in Atlanta, a few hours down the road. At the same time, while leading worship for the college ministry, I'd been writing worship music and toying with the idea of this becoming a vocational call. Now, through a series of God-orchestrated events, we'd been invited to move to Johns Creek, a suburb of Atlanta, to join the staff of Perimeter.

We were both familiar with their ministry, having heard founding pastor Randy Pope teach at a college conference. His teaching on discipleship forever changed how we understood ministry and the purpose of life in general. So when we got the seemingly random call to be part of Perimeter, we were like kids in a candy shop. We had won the employment jackpot! We couldn't pack up and sell our Spartanburg house fast enough—which was ultimately the problem.

We loved that little dump. We loved our third- and fourth-hand furniture and the curtains I'd sewn by hand when we were too broke to buy blinds. But we didn't think anyone else would have nearly as fond an affection for our home. So when the local college offered to buy it for above our asking price (I'm pretty sure they made it into a parking lot), we literally sold it out from under ourselves. The closing date for our Spartanburg house was May 31, but our start date at Perimeter wasn't until September 1. On June 1, with our few earthly possessions shoved in a five-by-ten-foot storage unit, we officially became homeless for three months.

A buddy of ours offered us an interim youth ministry position in the neighboring town of Greenville, South Carolina, but after we'd been on the job a couple of weeks, the housing situation attached to the position fell through. Desiring to be true to his word, our new pastor friend committed to finding us lodging. I'm pretty sure he put out a call to the entire congregation, begging families to take us, if even just for a week at a time.

Looking back now I can laugh at our situation. Some of the homes where we house-sat had hot tubs or fabulous mountain views, while others were more . . . interesting. One place had seven cats we were in charge of feeding while the owners were away. Of course we didn't mind, but we realized quickly that the cats weren't too keen on the idea that we were responsible for their well-being. We were pretty sure they were plotting to kill us in our sleep. In each case we were beyond thankful for a bed and a roof over our heads, but oh, how sweet it was to pull up to our newly purchased two-bedroom, twelve-hundred-square-foot townhome in Johns Creek. No more packed bags, no more cats; we were finally home.

Being between homes doesn't feel normal to most of us, but

it has often been very much the norm for God's people. The New Testament refers to Christians as *pilgrims* or *sojourners*. The apostle Paul wrote in his letter to the believers in Philippi that their citizenship was in heaven (Phil. 3:20). Peter's letters addressed how the Christians' conduct should be "during the time of your stay on earth" (1 Peter 1:17 NASB). Other versions translate this "throughout the time of your exile" (ESV) or living as "temporary residents" (NLT). From this we can know that since we are citizens of another kingdom, this earth is not our home.

What Martin and I felt during our short relocation experience, the people of Israel felt as well—many times, in fact. That's why God's promise to Abraham, Isaac, Jacob, Noah, Moses, and others was such a rich promise. He promised them land. And not just any land, but land with fertile soil, land to grow a nation on, land upon which to fulfill his promise of a great nation. A place that would provide for that great nation through agricultural blessing and safety from surrounding people groups. God promised Israel a home.

But obtaining this home wasn't as easy as downloading a Zillow app and signing a mortgage agreement. For the Israelites, accepting God's promised land was a long process involving a great journey and more blood, sweat, and tears than they ever could have envisioned.

An integral piece in understanding the Israelites' journey home is the story of their deliverance from Egypt. Before the animated feature *The Prince of Egypt* was released, you may have seen the older movie version of the story *The Ten Commandments*, with Charlton Heston starring as Moses. Remember the dramatic showdown between Heston and Yul Brynner? After Heston flexes his muscles and says, "Let my people go!" there's a bunch of special effects, and Israel is delivered! But this cinematic display glossed over two major themes of the book of Exodus.

One was the heart of the people. The other was the heart of God.

Longing for Home

Surveying the book of Exodus is a bit of a roller-coaster ride, with Israel's commitment to God reminiscent of that of a lovestruck middle school girl. There wasn't much consistency. But I'm often thankful that rather than telling a story about a people who were always confident, agreeable, and grateful, God tells us a story about a people more like me. I follow God much better when he gives me a map beforehand to let me know where I am going; and, when I make a turn I don't necessarily agree with, I'm rarely silent about my dissatisfaction with his chosen route. The truth is, I want to trust God whatever he asks of me, but sometimes my desire for comfort and familiarity gets the best of me. But enough about me. Back to Israel.

As the book begins, the nation of Israel was being held captive in Egypt. Flipping back a few pages, we can trace their captivity to the story of Joseph. After doing some serious apologizing for selling him into slavery, Joseph's brothers brought their families to live in the land of Goshen during a famine. But after the days of Joseph, who had favor with the pharaoh, a new king rose to power. The text says he "did not know Joseph" (Ex. 1:8). So as he looked out over his kingdom and saw how the Israelites had increased in numbers, this new pharaoh feared their growing presence (vv. 9–10). To control this perceived threat, he declared the Israelites slaves, "[making] their lives bitter with hard service, in mortar and brick" (v. 14).

Not only were the Israelites now a people oppressed but they were also victims of genocide. "Every son that is born to the Hebrews you shall cast into the Nile," the midwives were told (v. 22). Thanks to some God-fearing women, Moses' life was spared, and God orchestrated the opportunity for him to be raised by Pharaoh's daughter in the royal palace. But the hearts of God's people during those days were desperate.

The people of Israel groaned because of their slavery and cried out for help. Their cry for rescue from slavery came up to God. And God heard their groaning, and God remembered his covenant with Abraham, with Isaac, and with Jacob. God saw the people of Israel—and God knew. (2:23–25)

We don't see just the heart of the Israelites in this passage. We glimpse the heart of God. God heard the cries of his people. He saw their need for rescue and cared about their longing for a true home. Though Israel may have felt forgotten, God remembered them.

Ever wonder why the all-knowing God of the universe displayed what seemed like a memory lapse? Unlike us, God doesn't forget where he put his car keys or have to wear yesterday's socks again because he forgot to do laundry. God is not forgetful in the way we are. I love how R. Alan Cole explains it:

> He is the God who "remembered his covenant with Abraham" and with the other patriarchs. . . . To say that God "remembers" is an anthropomorphism . . . to express the changelessness of God. . . . To Hebrew thought, "to remember" is "to act." This too is equally applicable to God or to Israel. . . . God, says Scripture, "remembered Noah" (Gen. 8:1); that is to say, God acted in such a way to Noah as to show the consistency of his character. . . . So, to say that God "remembers" is to assert that he repeats his acts of saving grace towards his people Israel again and again, and in this way fulfils his promises, and shows his own self-consistency.[1]

Cole describes God's faithfulness as his "self-consistency." God is always moved by the broken hearts of his people because this is who he is. It is impossible for him to respond in a way that is inconsistent with his own character. God shows compassion because he *is* compassion. God initiates rescue because God is Rescuer. God is always who he is.

His consistency and care should give us confidence whenever we find ourselves feeling abandoned and forgotten—or homeless. Or unequal to the journey he's assigned to us.

God is always moved by the broken hearts of his people because this is who he is.

Moses was assigned a great hero moment, to confront Pharaoh. But to be true to Scripture, our hero was reluctant. Yet after Moses' burning-bush encounter and a pep talk from God, he stood before Pharaoh with a message from the Lord: "Let My people go" (Ex. 5:1 NASB).

When Moses asked for Israel's release, Pharaoh responded not only with a firm *no* but with a brute show of force, increasing the slaves' workload. In turn, the people of Israel became angry at Moses, and Moses questioned God about sending him in the first place. Yet again, God charged Moses with the task of delivering Israel. Pharaoh still refused, and the plagues began. You would think the first few plagues would have been enough to cause Pharaoh to reconsider and take this God that Moses represented a little more seriously. Maybe Pharaoh was cool with frogs in his bed and his entire nation going vegan.

But ultimately, God's display of power and fury proved too overwhelming for Egypt, and when the final plague resulted in the death of Pharaoh's firstborn—a penalty he'd been fine letting others experience but had never felt himself until then—Israel was released. After the Israelites had called Egypt home for more than four hundred years, God saw to it that they left with provisions in hand, even jewels. Grateful for a God who remembers, who rescues, and who keeps his promises, the people of Israel set out on a journey for home.

Unwelcome Detours

Just because we answer God's nudge to move out from our comfort zones—the familiar town, the community in which we raised our kids, whatever our idea of "home" is—doesn't mean the journey will be easy. It's easy to think that if I move forward in obedience, I'll be showered with blessings every step of the journey. Yet leaving is rarely painless, even if it's the right thing. And as I've sung more times that I can remember, the blessings God gives us aren't always the ones we anticipate!

Although the Israelites left Egypt with hearts full of faith, gleefully expectant of what God would do for them, this sentiment of hope and anticipation of a better life was short-lived. Where God's memory was long, their memories proved to be incredibly short. Following a cloud by day and a pillar of fire by night must have seemed to the Israelites a miraculous way to be led—that is, until they came to a dead end (Ex. 14). No motion-picture rendering could do the next scene justice.

The Lord had led them, *intentionally*, to this perilous spot. Six hundred Egyptian chariots hemmed them in on one side, and an enormous body of water on the other. Even Pharaoh's assessment of the Israelites' position was that the wilderness had "shut them in" (v. 3 NASB). As Pharaoh's confidence rose, theirs fell like a stone. Rather than lifting their eyes expectantly for what God was about to do, or reminding one another that God always sees his rescue plans through, they responded in fear. Yes, they cried out to God, but their greater cry was directed toward Moses. "Is it because there were no graves in Egypt that you have taken us away to die in the wilderness? Why have you dealt with us in this way, bringing us out of Egypt?" And perhaps the saddest of all indictments, "It would have been better for us to serve the Egyptians than to die in the wilderness" (vv. 11–12 NASB).

It would have been better if we were still slaves in Egypt than about to die here in the wilderness. This statement is so heartbreaking to me. Despite God's show of power, the Israelites doubted his promise to bring them safely home. Rather than evaluating their current predicament based on what they had always held to be true about God, they changed their view based on their circumstances.

Ever been tempted to respond this way? Your bills are piling up, so you question whether God really is Provider. You're chastised for your faith at work or school, and you wonder whether God really is Defender. You feel alone, and you wonder whether the God who promised never to leave or forsake you is really with you. To be human is to doubt.

And that was where the Israelites found themselves, allowing their circumstances to lessen their view of their God. They failed to see him as Rescuer. They failed to see him as all-powerful. They failed to see him as faithful.

Now, I do want to give them some grace here. They had been living in a foreign culture for more than four hundred years. Perhaps their understanding of God had diminished over the generations. My sadness for the Israelites is genuine because I, too, can forget that God is faithful to his promises.

Fear often makes us lose sight of the great God who loves us and delivers us moment by moment.

Tempted to Settle

In the Exodus story, we see that the human heart has a difficult time leaving normal, if for no other reason than simply because it is familiar. Like the Israelites' captivity in Egypt, our circumstances may not be ideal, but when they're all we know, they become our normal. Remember here again that we were created for security and stability, for wholeness. That explains why our hearts have a hard time moving away from them.

We see this in how the Israelites' momentary discomfort sweetened their memories of slave life in Egypt. I wish I could say that after the incredible way they were delivered through the parting of the Red Sea, their doubts disappeared. But if you skip ahead a few chapters, you'll read of more doubt, more grumblings, and unfortunately, more misremembering and embellishing of their home in Egypt. "Would that we had died by the hand of the LORD in the land of Egypt," they complained, "when we sat by the meat pots and ate bread to the full" (Ex. 16:3).

Do I highlight this to shame Israel for their poor short-term memory? No, I say it to highlight a tendency I see in myself as well.

Think about this. The people were carrying Joseph's bones with them. After Israel's centuries-long enslavement, anyone who knew life prior to Egypt now resided in a casket. The people may have heard stories about the home God had promised—*Are those stories even true?* they may have wondered—but all they knew themselves was slavery. And facing their Red Sea moment, they would have chosen slavery over the unknown.

As the dust cloud of the advancing Egyptians neared, the choice seemed easy. Reality overcame wishful thinking. Doubt paralyzed. Slavery became preferable to freedom.

The Israelites couldn't dream big enough to imagine what God was about to do.

Look at your own life today. Consider its normal patterns that provide a sense of stability for you and your family. These aren't bad at all. Routine allows us to avoid chaos, which seems always to be knocking at our doors. Life in a normal environment can foster a sense of love and appreciation in us. I know it does in me.

But if normal is our goal, our highest value—or to take it a little to the dark side, our addiction—we may very well miss the extraordinary work God has in store. Just like Israel, we may be choosing the bondage of normal over the promise of better things. Hard as it is to believe, freedom and deliverance, unlike anything we could imagine, often await us if we will only trust the God who rescues.

We may be choosing the bondage of normal over the promise of better things.

What normal patterns are you unwilling to release? Are you remaining in an unhealthy relationship out of comfort or convenience? Have you been allowing areas of complacency or sin to remain, simply because they've become normalized? Are you partaking in actions or behaviors that are normal for the people around you when you know God's been calling you to something different?

Often our idea of normal comes from our families of origin. We may have been raised to act or be a certain way. When asked, "Why do you do that?" our response is, "It's the way we have always done it." Or maybe, "We have always believed this."

Staying in normal for the sake of normal may be shortchanging the very purpose of your life—to embark on a journey with a delivering Savior who came to bring you *new* life!

Our True Dwelling Place

When we left the Israelites standing on the shore of the Red Sea, they were murmuring and complaining, wishing they could go back to Egypt. But something incredible happened: God came through for his people. Even when they doubted, God delivered. Even when they strayed, God remained ever faithful.

Their God—their Rescuer, their Deliverer, the God of the universe who was their Champion—parted the Red Sea. They crossed on dry land. And once they were on the other side, Pharaoh and his army drowned in the very waters that parted for the Israelites. Talk about interesting dinner conversation!

Much later Moses would look back with clarity on these events and the years of wilderness wandering that followed. Long after the burning bush, the showdown with Pharaoh, and decades of nomadic living while longing for the promised land, he penned Psalm 90. His words speak of a greater home.

> Lord, you have been our dwelling place
> > in all generations.
> Before the mountains were brought forth,
> > or ever you had formed the earth and the world,
> > from everlasting to everlasting you are God. (vv. 1–2)

Doesn't this sound like an important epiphany? Moses' conclusion was this: You, oh Lord, are our dwelling place! *You* are our home! Yes, we are traveling toward a place that is the fulfillment of your promise, but even as we travel, you are our home. While enduring torture at the hand of the Egyptians, you were our home in Egypt. When we feared certain death by Pharaoh's army, you were our home by the Red Sea. As we followed a cloud by day and a pillar of fire by night, you were our home in our wandering. No matter our geographic location, you were always and forever will be home to your people.

Israel's dwelling place wasn't a destination but the constant presence of a faithful God!

What does this mean for us? Seeing God as our home means we no longer let our routines, the status quo of those around us, or the patterns handed down to us by our parents dictate our comfort or stand in the way of following God's lead. We can throw normal to the wind because our home is not a place; our home is a person! And not just any person. Psalm 90 tells us he is the maker of the heavens and earth! "From everlasting to everlasting [he is] God." I cannot think of a more stable place to rest. Our home is in a person who has no beginning and no end—nor does his faithfulness to his children.

My Moses moment arrived when I became pregnant with our first child, Josie. Little did Martin and I know that a song I'd written six months earlier, one that started as a private, very personal journal entry, was making its way onto radio airwaves and was about to open doors to many speaking and concert events across the nation. As elated as I was to begin accepting these invitations, I was growing more concerned with each passing month of my pregnancy. Intellectually, I knew that God's timing was perfect—but, really, did he have to wait until I was expecting my first child for my touring career to take off?

I considered that God might be testing me to see whether I would be willing to give up a recording career for family. But the more I prayed about the pregnancy and the growing ministry opportunities, the more I became confident God wanted me to do both. Like Moses, I hesitatingly agreed. I stepped forward in obedience, trusting that God would show me how to be a good mom, even away from home. I'm still stunned by the privilege it was—and still is—to play that song, "Blessings," night after night.

As I look through photos of raising our family on the road, I see nothing normal about it. Nothing screams abnormal like those first couple of years with Josie. For one thing, we visited forty-eight states in eighteen months, which must have set a world record! She napped in my guitar case. She stood next to me at huge arena events wearing big pink protective earmuffs, mesmerized by all the haze and flashing lights. When the headliner invited me onstage to play a few songs, I'd hand her off to the guy running monitors, one of many tech guys we referred to as her "tour uncles." As an almost-two-year-old, she helped the Compassion International rep set out packets about needy little boys and girls from all over the world, calling each one "baby" as she set them on the table.

Some days we played at churches where she had the entire nursery wing to herself. Other days she picked animal hair off her onesie inside dusty arenas that had played host to a rodeo the night before. We traveled with a small bag of toys, a few books, and a high chair (when I remembered it). We were far from home, in every sense of the word. Yet those were such sweet days that the mere memories bring tears to my eyes as I type.

You may read this with great concern, since what I just described goes against every parenting blog about safety and stability in a child's formative years. If that's what you're thinking, you may want to stop reading now, because the upcoming chapters are filled with unconventional parenting stories!

For us, those memories of Josie traveling with me are tiny snapshots of a big God protecting our family. But he also birthed in Josie, at a young age, an understanding of his mission. God sustained us. He met every one of our needs. Though Josie's first two years weren't spent at home, they were spent in the home we made for her. Martin and I were her dwelling place, and God was ours. We were Josie's stability. Each night she slept in a different bed, but it was always right between the two humans who loved her more than anything on the face of the earth. We were her home. And in each photo, her goofy, toothless smile confirms that the home we provided was enough.

What is *your* dwelling place?

Perhaps God has physically displaced you, calling you from the place you thought of as home to a new place of residence. More often, God simply calls us out from the familiar. And when we make God our dwelling place, we can accept whatever earthly home or new circumstances he calls us to. We let the comforts of this world off the hook, believing that the longings of our hearts can be met not by a place but by a person.

Has God called you to move to a lower-income area to share your abundance with those in need? Has he called you to move closer to someone familiar, someone with whom you have been estranged, to become a caregiver or to build a relational bridge? Or maybe God is calling you to leave something behind, but the final destination is still unknown. You are in good company: when Jesus called his first disciples, he gave them no more instruction than, "Follow me!" (Mark 1:17).

Jesus calls all his disciples to live as sojourners in a world that isn't quite home. Still, we don't have to feel afraid or abandoned. *He* is our dwelling place. He always has been, and he always will be.

Josie never truly left home because Martin and I were her dwelling place. Moses came to a similar realization. God was his dwelling place.

In all our Moses moments, whenever God takes us to the shore of the Red Sea, and a dust cloud of fear threatens to overwhelm us, may we be reminded that he is right there with us. In those instances, may we come to a place of saying "So long, home," and find our dwelling place in God alone.

So Long, Normal Story

The Roland Family

Meet the Rolands

After a dozen years of marriage, John and Whitney Roland of Atlanta, Georgia, left normal behind. For two years, they traveled the country in an RV with their daughters, Wylie and Lola, ages thirteen and twelve, and their toy fox terrier, Chloe.

Laura: Describe the normal you used to know.

John: Before we took this big step, I was working full-time as a videographer at a church, and Whitney was working as a freelance artist. Our lives were pretty normal.

Whitney: Yep, we did the normal suburban-parents thing. School, activities, church, et cetera.

Laura: What happened that caused you to say so long to normal?

Whitney: What first began the shift was some trouble one of our daughters was having in school. After we saw her struggle with subjects she had loved in the past, Wylie was finally diagnosed with dyslexia. As we navigated this with her school, John kept suggesting, "Why don't you consider homeschooling?"

John: To give you a bit of background, when Whitney and I got engaged fourteen years ago, she had two conditions upon which we would marry. She wanted to name our first child Wylie, and she never, ever, ever wanted to homeschool! Those were her two deal breakers!

Whitney: Fast-forward to many years later. One day Wylie and I were at home working on homework, both of us in tears, and it was as if I heard God say, *Why don't you homeschool?* From then on, my attitude changed a bit toward the idea. I began to think, *Just maybe.* And it was around that time John began to research families who were homeschooling . . . in an RV.

John: Another piece of the story was that my job changed from being on site, full-time, to contract. It was as if God was paving the way to take our family on this amazing adventure. And we didn't want to look back and wonder why we missed such an incredible opportunity.

Whitney: We also have a family motto that we've always tried to live by. We'd rather try, even if we fail, than never try at all. So, we did it. We had no idea what we were doing, but we did it. We bought an RV, planned a course, and hit the road.

Laura: Wow! After making the decision, did you ever ask yourselves, "What have we done?"

Whitney: A thousand times! For our first trip, we made ourselves go from Atlanta to Maine. We wanted to be too far away to chicken out! There were days when we thought we would lose our minds. One very rainy day, John was working remotely from a Dunkin' Donuts, and the girls and I sat in the RV and just cried, missing home. But each day something reminded us of why God had called us on this journey. But initially, it was a big step of faith.

Laura: What has been your steady?

John: Our faith, first of all. Part of our motivation in the beginning was getting our girls out in creation, so that they might be wowed by what God has made. Rather than just seeing it in books, we took them to see the mountains of Yosemite and the canyons of Arizona. We showed them the works of God's hands and talked with them about it, helping them process how big and amazing God truly is.

Whitney: And the uniqueness of his creation! Through the National Park Service Junior Ranger program, we learned about weather patterns and how God equipped different animals to live in different climates. All four of us were awed each day by what we saw. We even had the chance to visit some churches that looked way different than what we'd experienced. I'll never forget visiting a church on our Alaska trip. You could only get there by boat, and it was in someone's house! But the kindness of the people made us feel right at home. I loved that our kids got to see that even church can look different from the one they grew up in.

Laura: What has been your gain?

Lola: We definitely learned to go with the flow!

Whitney: People often asked how we could stand being in such a small space with each other for such a long time. Honestly, it forced us to learn how to communicate. When you have an argument, you can't storm out of a room when you are living in a one-room RV! Really, I cannot stress how much closer we grew as a family. We learned to work together, problem solving both logistically and relationally. And that is a tool we will lean on in the future as a family, on or off the road.

John: It's hard for me to fully know yet how this has impacted me. My main motivation, even from the beginning, was knowing that our girls aren't going to stay young forever. Life gets busy. Kids grow up. When I think of the memories we've made . . . it brings tears to my eyes.

Whitney: And our experience has completely changed how I view our "at home" life. I feel a lot freer to make changes in our normal day to day. If something's not working for our family, scrap it. Try something different. We're not married to one way of doing something. We don't have to follow the same path everyone else is following. And our decisions don't have to make sense to everyone else. We've taught our girls that it's okay to think outside the box. If God's calling you to something extraordinary, take that leap!

Laura: So now you are back living in the "normal," but it sounds like you are no longer attached to it. Is that right?

John: Yeah, the principle isn't that you should sell everything, quit your job and your school, and hit the road in an RV. It's about figuring out what that thing is for *you*! Is there something God's calling you to that you've been too scared to try? Maybe you're afraid of what others would think, or afraid you don't have what it takes. Will you have the faith to follow God on whatever adventure he's calling you to?

Chapter Four

So Long, Self

I got caught in a blizzard traveling back to Grand Rapids from Chicago with some college friends. We had to spend the night huddled up in a Honda Accord at a truck stop. This southern girl had no idea what *lake-effect snow* meant until that night, or how seriously one should take the meteorologist's warning!

I usually make it a point not to go to Michigan in January, since I'm not a huge fan of driving on snow in flimsy compact rental cars (I always go for the cheapest option). But I found myself there this past winter, kicking off the new year with a women's conference in Grand Rapids. Being there in and of itself brought back quite a few memories.

Years earlier, I had attended Calvin College (now Calvin University) as a freshman, but after one cold semester I ended up back home. I won't go into all the details, but it was my first time living on my own. Let's just say that the strong faith I thought I had as a nineteen-year-old could not withstand the temptations of college life. After three months of partying, sneaking in after dorm curfews, and lying to my resident assistant about where I had been, God brought conviction to my heart in a heavy way. It was our final week of classes, and a few of us had gone to an off-campus party to celebrate right before exams. (Let me assure you that I now realize this doesn't make a whole lot of sense, and that taking my exams after a mere three hours of sleep was not likely to increase my chances of passing.)

As we arrived back on campus, a few resident assistants smelled the sweet aroma of partying on us. They banished us to our rooms, where we awaited punishment. What made things far worse for me was a comment from my dorm director. He wasn't mad, though he certainly wasn't happy with me either. He simply looked at me with kindness in his eyes. "Laura," he said, "you are better than this." His words were nonjudgmental. He was just speaking the truth I already knew to be true in my heart.

I was created for more than the people-pleasing partying I had been involved in. I didn't need to be popular or cool. Even though the party scene was considered the "normal" college experience, I knew I was created for more.

So now here I was, headed to Grand Rapids for this conference. A few months earlier, I had met a fellow worship leader named John Witvliet at a conference. To call John a worship leader is a bit of an understatement. His writing on worship is a true gift to the church—in fact, he has authored textbooks that are used in colleges and seminaries around the world. I had read a few of John's books and told him that I'd love to connect and talk more, to which he responded, "If you are ever up in Grand Rapids, I teach at Calvin, and we'd love for you to come by!" Of all the places he could have worked, really? Calvin? I had not set foot on that campus since my incredibly shameful freshman year, and I wasn't even sure security would allow me back.

I accepted John's invitation and made plans to arrive early for my conference and have coffee with John and a few of his colleagues. As we set up the meeting on the phone, there were a few moments that must have struck him as odd.

"Do you know where we are located?" John asked.

"Yes," I sheepishly answered. "I actually attended Calvin the first semester of my freshman year."

"Really?" John answered with surprise. "I had no idea!"

Yeah, they probably had it expunged from their records, I thought.

"Well, my office is in the library, so just text me when you get here."

"Okay, great . . . and where is the library?" Long awkward pause.

I pulled onto Calvin's campus and headed to the library for the first time in my life. I trembled a bit as I got out of my car and set foot in a place I had vowed never to return to. I grabbed baby Tim and his stroller from the back seat. Nothing says "I'm not a student" like bringing a baby with you to campus. Strangely, having Tim with me helped remind me that I wasn't that lost college student anymore. I was fighting to believe it, anyway.

We began walking along the path to this elusive library John had spoken of. On the way, I passed my old dorm. There was the tree I stood under when I lied to my suitemates about where I was going that one weekend. There were the buildings housing the classes my parents paid hard-earned money for me to attend, classes I'd either blown off or attended with apathy. I'd been so blind to what a gift an education was.

With every step I felt more shame. My long-ago decisions could never be changed. My relationships with those people could never be repaired. I had rightfully earned the opinions people formed about me with my immoral and reckless behavior. And as I walked those steps, not really knowing how to pray, I felt my lips whispering, "Jesus, be near. Jesus, be near." It was all I could say.

Have you ever revisited a place that caused you to feel shame? Have you ever had to walk a path, enter a building, or encounter a group of people that brought to mind an earlier chapter of your life story that you prefer would stay closed for good? If so, you are not alone.

Obsessed with Self

I have a child who hates brushing her hair. I'm trying to keep this anonymous so as not to embarrass her, but since I only have one daughter, you can figure it out. I'll ask her to brush her hair in the morning before school, and every day she has the same response: "It looks fine!"

Really? Maybe for a caveman or someone who lives in a barn!

What I am really asking is for Josie to be a little more self-aware. And at the same time, one thing I love about Josie is that she isn't. She hasn't begun the rat race that we adults constantly engage in, the struggle against constantly thinking of self. I love theologian Tim Keller's definition of *humility*. This was a monumental truth for me to learn, and it would be even more life-changing if I could live it out. He simply says, "The essence of gospel-humility is not thinking more of myself or thinking less of myself, it is thinking of myself less."[1] Why is it I am so obsessed with me? Why is my greatest struggle in life either thinking too highly of myself or being overly critical and thinking too lowly of myself? Maybe it's time for a good old-fashioned breakup.

One of my favorite things about Bart Millard is his ability to sing about deep theological truths in a pithy and fun way. Bart is the lead singer of the contemporary Christian band MercyMe, writer of the hit song "I Can Only Imagine," and recipient of many awards and accolades. MercyMe and I are also on the same record label, so I've been privileged to share the stage with them many times. But what always stands out about Bart is not his theological depth, although he definitely has that, but his fun-loving spirit.

Always a bit of a jokester, Bart has a jovial approach to even the deepest topics that helps him gently deliver poignant messages. His song "So Long Self"[2] is a perfect example of this. If you haven't heard it, you need to give it a listen. He compares our obsession with self to a dating relationship in which we are completely smitten with me, myself, and I. Then comes the farewell, in which Bart proceeds to break up with himself, like someone dumping their high school sweetheart right before leaving for college. He claims he has found someone else and must bid himself goodbye. It makes me laugh every time.

But as humorous as his take is on his relationship with self, there isn't one of us who can't relate on some level. It seems there is nobody I love more than me, although somehow there is also no harsher critic of myself than me.

When we consider saying goodbye to normal, let's be honest: there is nothing more normal than putting ourselves first. Whether it is choosing what to have for dinner, agreeing on which movie to see with our spouses on date night (the chick flick or that generic underdog sports movie—same plot, different sport every time), or thinking our schedules are more important than those of everyone else stuck in this traffic jam, we are all afflicted with these tendencies.

Thinking of ourselves first is so ingrained in us that you might even say we were born with it. I have a pretty adorable example of this theory living right here in my house. His name is Timothy, and he is my fourth child. At just two years of age, Timmy can already say *helicopter, meatball, playground, Alexa,* and many other useful words. But there's one word he can't say, or maybe just won't. He literally cannot say his own name, Timothy. When the supermarket clerk says, "Hey, cutie! What's your name?" Timmy replies, "My."

He calls himself My. As you can imagine, this is pretty adorable. But in those moments when he becomes adamant about claiming his territory, the adorableness quickly wears off. There is no longer a toy in our home that is not "My!" There is not a bed, whether already occupied at 2:00 a.m. or not, that doesn't instantly become "My!" Any cookie, chip, gummy, raisin, or Milk Dud that has yet to be ingested is "My!" And heaven forbid another child tries to sit in my lap. Timmy will full-on, WWE-style body-slam me, while squealing at decibels only dogs can hear, "Myyyyyyyy!"

He loves his stuff. He loves to lay claim to other people's stuff. He loves to get his way. And the only difference between him and me is that he doesn't even try to hide his selfish desire to lay claim to everything! I may possess sophisticated social skills that allow me to mask it, but the root desire is the same. There is no bigger fan of me . . . than me.

How is it that we have become so obsessed with ourselves? And why is this accepted as normal in our culture—so normal, in fact, that it's the foundation for the elusive American dream? We are raised to believe the definition of success is to work hard, achieve, and acquire. As Ricky Bobby says in the movie *Talladega Nights*, "If you ain't first, you're last."[3] Sure, our culture prizes philanthropy, but only from our excess. We give out of our surplus, after first gaining for ourselves. But what is it about human nature that desperately dictates we fill our lives with shiny stuff and cool people and the praise of others? Where does the drive to think of self first come from?

As I try to understand the energy behind this relentless pursuit, I am reminded that our struggle is nothing new. As we saw in chapter 1, the normal that existed at the time God brought creation into existence has been distorted. We saw how all order began to unravel in the story of creation in the early chapters of Genesis. What happened all the way back in the garden continues to play out even today. Adam and Eve wondered if they were living as fully as they should, thanks to an element of doubt introduced by the serpent. They began to question whether God was being completely honest with them. Was it possible he was holding out on them?

The Antidote to Both Pride and Shame

As we dig deeper into what it means to say so long to self, we'll begin someplace that may seem unlikely. I believe the key to breaking the cycle of being wrapped up in ourselves is properly understanding the heart of the gospel. If I asked a dozen people what the gospel is, I am sure I would get a dozen different answers. Each answer might state a portion of it accurately, but my experience suggests the responses would leave us wanting. I'll try to provide a definition that is simple yet comprehensive enough to give us a solid understanding of the meaning of this common Christian term.

Most Greek lexicons define "the gospel" as "good news." It comes from the Greek word *evangelion*. In his book *The Gospel*, Ray Ortlund points out that "the gospel is not law, demanding that we pay our own way. [It] is a welcome announcement, declaring that Jesus paid it all."[4]

Surely this is good news.

> The key to breaking the cycle of being wrapped up in ourselves is properly understanding the heart of the gospel.

Think about news we encounter every day, usually in the form of the spoken word accompanied by visual images. The good news of the gospel is similar in some respects. It is specific content that comes to us from the Bible. The content of the Bible as a whole comes in the form of history, poetry, songs, parables, and complex theology. Through each different work we see a golden thread connecting them all. That thread is God's saving work through Jesus—the gospel.

Paul explained the gospel and its importance in 1 Corinthians 15:

> Now I make known to you, brothers and sisters, the gospel which I preached to you, which also you received, in which also you stand, by which you also are saved, if you hold fast the word which I preached to you, unless you believed in vain.
>
> For I handed down to you as of first importance what I also received, that Christ died for our sins according to the Scriptures, and that He was buried, and that He was raised on the third day according to the Scriptures, and that He appeared to Cephas, then to the twelve. After that He appeared to more than five hundred brothers and sisters at one time, most of whom remain until now, but some have fallen asleep. (vv. 1–6 NASB)

Let me make a couple of observations about this passage. First, Paul preached what he had received. He passed on to others the content that was given to him. In Paul's day, the gospel was meant to be passed on to others, and this remains true today. It was never Paul's to keep. Also, it did not originate with him. He did not cleverly create this message. It was of divine origin, and this is supported by the impact it had on the lives of those who received it.

Second, this gospel message was surrounded by proof elements. There were the many prophecies fulfilled in Jesus' life, ministry, and death. There was the resurrection—witnessed by more than five hundred people, many of whom were still living at the time Paul wrote this letter to the Corinthians. Finally, all that was done was done with the oversight of God the Father and the authority of Scripture. These are the principal elements of the good news of the gospel.

I have heard it taught that people who believe in God want to rightly relate to him. Or as my pastor Randy Pope likes to say, "Everyone wants God to like them."[5] They "perform" and they are counting on what they "do" to create a sufficient righteousness to earn God's favor. We refer to this earned righteousness as "self-righteousness."

But there is another way to relate to God—the way of Jesus, described by the word *grace*. The emphasis in this approach is acknowledging what has already been *done*. We don't depend on our merit to save us but rather the merit of the finished work of Christ. In this approach we experience the great exchange. Jesus takes our sin on himself, and he gives us his righteousness. But it doesn't end there.

Once our sins are forgiven and our debt has been paid by Christ himself on the cross, the question arises, What do we do now in recognition of this great act of grace and mercy? Because of the great love demonstrated by Christ, we are compelled to perform (2 Cor. 5:14).[6] We pursue righteousness no longer to earn God's favor but because he has loved and saved us.

Many of us, having lost sight of the simple understanding of the gospel of grace that points to Christ's deep love for us, have lost our contentment. So we pursue self-satisfaction instead. Our affections have been captured by illusions tied to success, fame, or financial security. We may have settled for contentment, or at least an imitation of contentment, as our life's goal. But to fully realize a life of contentment, we need to say goodbye to self and to all our efforts to earn right standing with God. Failure to do this will result in a life filled with disappointment.

It's been said that only the gospel of Jesus Christ gives "the verdict before the performance."[7] Can you imagine such grace? I saw this concept play out in real life once.

Many years ago, I was leading worship at a large conference, and slated to perform before my set was a small local worship band. When I met the guys backstage, it was immediately clear they had never played before an audience of this size. Quite frankly, they were terrified. Since I was also the emcee for the event, I walked to the front of the stage to introduce them and did something I'd never done before.

With the opening band still backstage, unable to hear what I was saying, I told the audience how excited I was to hear them and how much it would encourage them to receive a standing ovation *before* they even started playing. So as soon as I announced the band, the audience rose to their feet with thunderous applause. At first, the band was speechless. Then big grins spread across their faces. They went on to play their entire set without error. The pressure was off. The crowd had already voted, and it was unanimous: this band was a hit before they played their first note!

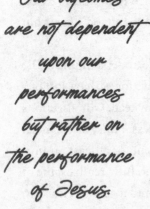
Our outcomes are not dependent upon our performances but rather on the performance of Jesus.

This is what I mean when I say the gospel gives us the verdict before the performance. God is crazy about you, and there's no amount of goodness or badness that would change that! If we have accepted the good news of the gospel and entrusted our lives to him, our outcomes are not dependent on our performances but rather on the performance of Jesus.

That's the grace we've been given.

Under Construction

The transformative truth of God's grace became particularly meaningful for me this year as I carried Timmy in his stroller up those library steps at Calvin, whispering and pleading with Jesus to be near. It turned out that was all I needed to say. This was one of a handful of moments in my life when I've felt grace so tangibly that it wrapped my weary body like a warm blanket.

God's grace met me between Beets-Veenstra and Noordewier-VanderWerp residence halls (yes, the college's founders were Dutch) and reminded me that it wasn't my squeaky-clean track record that garnered God's affection for me. It wasn't back when I was an underperforming college freshman any more that it is today. Let's face it—if my hope depended on my own ability to gain acceptance and love from God, my hope was lost.

With each step, my shame was shaken off and replaced with Jesus' presence. Maybe I couldn't change what I had done that long-ago semester, but I no longer felt the need to wear that shame. Here was the truth that was coming to mean so much to me: Jesus didn't change those actions. They were what they were. Instead, he went a step further, and he took my shame upon himself. Imagine shame like a heavy backpack, like the one I would often wear on campus, filled with large hardback textbooks. Jesus lifted that load, not by minimizing it or even dismissing it as if it wasn't there; he simply removed the heavy weight from my shoulders and harnessed it upon himself. He bore the weight of my sin and my shame on the cross. Yes, I had always known this to be true theologically, but as I stood up straight, free from the weight of that load, I knew it to be true *actually*. Jesus was carrying my shame, and I was walking in freedom.

And the most amazing process unfolded. Jesus changed me. He

changed my heart, my emotions, and that little recording that had long been playing in my mind. Rather than hearing the accusations of the Evil One saying, "You are disgraceful and scandalous, and you don't even know where the library is!" I began to hear the voice of my Savior: "You are a *new* creation. You are loved. You are mine."

This is my confidence, and I long for you to have it as well. Jesus is committed to doing a work within each of his disciples, changing us a little more each day. The theological word for this is *sanctification*, which simply means that God's plan is to leave no part of us unchanged. He changes our minds, our will, our behaviors, and our affections through the work of the Holy Spirit. Frankly, I'm excited about this. Of course, I love the TV show *Fixer Upper*. In the same way, you and I are under total renovation. This is God's transformative work, not ours. All we need to do is cooperate with him.

No one puts this better than Elyse Fitzpatrick, reflecting on the deepest implications of the gospel:

> True Christianity is not a program of self-improvement; it's an acknowledgment that something more than self-improvement is needed. What's needed is death and resurrection: gospel words, gospel constructs, gospel motives, gospel power—a loving Redeemer.[8]

While the world and our human nature compel us to focus on ourselves, to strive for acceptance and satisfaction by becoming good enough, strong enough, smart enough, and successful enough, Jesus offers another way. The good news of the gospel means that we can say so long to our obsession with self, goodbye to the endless swing between shaming ourselves for not measuring up and elevating ourselves and our desires as most important.

Praise God! We don't have to be enough. We simply need to believe that he is enough.

If Joni Eareckson Tada were here, she would probably end the chapter like this:

> My faith has found a resting place,
> Not in device nor creed;
> I trust the Everliving One,
> His wounds for me shall plead.
>
> Enough for me that Jesus saves,
> This ends my fear and doubt;
> A sinful soul I come to Him,
> He'll never cast me out.
>
> I need no other argument,
> I need no other plea;
> It is enough that Jesus died,
> And that He died for me.[9]

May your faith and your soul find its resting place in Jesus, trusting him with your past and believing he has good things in store for your future. He has redeemed you not only with a price but for a purpose.

Chapter Five

So Long, Identity

"Anyone up for going to Mongolia?" someone said.

Hmm. An alternative to working another summer at Pizza Inn. "Sure!" I replied.

This opportunity knocked at the end of my first term at the University of South Carolina, where I had landed after my brief, dubious stint at Calvin College. U of SC was only an hour and a half from my parents' home, and frankly I was done with being so far from familiar turf. What I really needed was a fresh start, and U of SC seemed like a good place to try to figure out what to do with my life. Through a series of God-orchestrated events, I started as a music major. But after breaking my arm, I had to drop out of most of my music performance classes.

And now, on an impulse, I'd just agreed to spend my summer with a nonprofit organization doing mission work in Mongolia. Yes, that's how aimless I was at nineteen.

It's hard to summarize what happened that summer in Outer Mongolia, but it is not an overstatement to say it was life changing. Imagine the camping scene at the end of *The Parent Trap*, either the

Hayley Mills or the Lindsay Lohan version. I lived for a solid month with seven other girls in a yurt. And when you think yurt, don't picture the glamping kind you see on Airbnb. This was a massive cloth tent we set up ourselves, in which we slept in sleeping bags on the cold, hard ground. We ate jelly and bread for most breakfasts and lunches, and some sort of mutton stew cooked over an open fire for dinner. We ate so much mutton I still cringe when I hear the sound of a sheep bleating.

But it's not an overstatement to say that I was transformed in Outer Mongolia, and in more ways than just my swearing off mutton for the rest of my existence. Our primary purpose was to share the gospel with the nomads, those tending their flocks on the hills. My life was profoundly impacted by this work.

To give you some context, this was a critical time in Mongolia's history. Mongolians were coming out from under the grip of Communism and undergoing important leadership changes within their country. Prior to that year, they had a handful of underground churches, but there had never been an opportunity to share one's faith openly without being harassed, or worse, by the government. We believed we were stepping through a door that generations before us had prayed would open. The harvest was ripe. Coming alongside the godly indigenous leaders already there, we shared the good news of the gospel with nomads, through translators.

I had grown up hearing this teaching in church my whole life. But now, sharing about Jesus' saving grace every day, I realized that my own understanding and appreciation of the gospel story was becoming true for me in a way it never had before. I began believing it in a deep way in my soul. The only way I can explain it is that what was once a big *part* of my life was now becoming the *very core* of who I was.

If you imagine a wagon wheel, my faith had always been a strong spoke. But during those weeks, God reprioritized my life. This was more than mere rearranging; it was as if he completely dismantled my wagon wheel and rebuilt it with himself as the hub. Jesus was no longer an activity or a passion; he was my reason for living.

And he was speaking a new identity over me.

I distinctly remember sitting on the side of one of those Outer Mongolian hills, completely perplexed. I had quite literally left everything behind. All my friends, my cute car, the musical instruments that had been so helpful in drawing attention and accolades to myself. I'd left my family and my church, which had been the greatest champions of my faith up to that point. I now possessed one backpack with two changes of clothes, a toothbrush, and a stick of deodorant, which was quickly wearing down. Yet in that moment I was happier than I had ever been. My arms were empty, but my heart was full.

As I sat on that hillside, watching the sun set over the stream I had done my laundry in for the past three weeks, considering the simple lifestyle of the nomads caring for their flocks, I knew everything had to change. I knew everything, for me, *was* changing.

Saying so long to self-focus, as we saw in the previous chapter, is an important step toward the freedom to be all we were created to be. And it leads to another step, another goodbye. We must leave behind our former identities and embrace a new identity in Christ.

For some of us, this change may be more dramatic than for others. For me, it meant leaving behind the self-focused way I'd been living the past year. It also meant cutting ties with the moral posing I'd been doing at my new school. I suppose I shouldn't have been surprised God would take me to the other side of the world, to a most unusual environment, in order to call me away from the "normal" identity I'd been pursuing. That's how serious he was about giving me a new identity.

What Is *Identity*?

When you consider the word *identity*, what comes to mind? If, like me, you enjoy spy movies, you might immediately think of a double agent. Or maybe a superhero concealing who he or she is in real life. Most dictionaries define *identity* as the distinguishing character or personality of an individual.

But the identity I'm thinking about encompasses more than simply concealing one's self from others. Our identity is who we believe we are, and it affects how we portray ourselves to others. It's amazing how much time and money we spend over a lifetime trying to maintain or alter or improve how we see ourselves and how others view us. Image management is a billion-dollar industry, consisting of makeup and lotions that claim to be age defying, as well as exceedingly uncomfortable clothing that attempts to conform our bodies into someone's ideal. (Spanx, I'm looking at you!)

During the COVID-19 quarantine, I was asked to make a video for an upcoming event that had been moved from in person to online. I came home afterward all dolled up. This was the first time my kids had seen me in anything other than sweatpants for months. "Mom! You look so beautiful!" Ben said. "On the outside, I mean. I'm not sure about the inside."

And it's the truth. When I consider why I dress up for a concert or speaking engagement, it is because I care what you think of me. Specifically, I care what you think about how I look. I've been known to wear boots with a small heel and fitted jeans because I was told this was slenderizing, particular for a woman who has had four children. Apparently I care about more than just whether my songs deliver encouraging truth; I want you to like me.

Most of us wear things, say things, and do things in an effort to manage others' opinions. We all care about our identities.

Caring about how others view us isn't wrong (especially if it motivates us to shower a few times a week). But when others' perceptions begin to rule our lives, when we find ourselves crippled by someone's negative opinion or even enslaved to keeping up a certain image, we've been set up for failure. We don't need to exhaust ourselves physically or mentally, running a race that Christ already completed on our behalf.

But what does it look like tangibly to let go of our identities, to not be defined by our roles in life, even the good ones? How might one attain this freedom from caring what others think? It certainly sounds like an incredibly liberating place to live. But how exactly do we get there? Is such a destination even within our reach?

> *We don't need to exhaust ourselves physically or mentally, running a race that Christ already completed on our behalf.*

God Pursues Us

The story of Hagar shows us that when we come to the end of ourselves, we usually find that God's plan for us is just beginning. Hagar's story, found in Genesis 16, is not very long, but it really captures my heart.

The chapter begins with a different woman, Sarai, who bemoaned the fact that she was childless even though God promised her husband he would father many nations (Gen. 12). She was in her seventies, what doctors these days might call of "advanced maternal age." I know this term well, since I had three kids after age thirty-five. It should be no shock to anyone that Sarai was having trouble getting pregnant in her seventies. In light of this setback, and thinking God needed some help in executing his promise, she came up with a plan.

She told her husband, Abram, "'Behold now, the LORD has prevented me from bearing children. Go in to my servant; it may be that I shall obtain children by her.' And Abram listened to the voice of Sarai" (16:2). I should probably skip any off-color jokes about how Abram finally started listening to his wife. Okay, maybe just one. Imagine Sarai thinking, *He never hears me when I ask him to take out the trash, but this time, he listens?!*

This entire situation was depraved on so many levels. First, consider Sarai. She was childless and desperate. In her culture, infertility wasn't just disappointing and shameful; the inability to bear your husband a child was a blow to your very identity. Biblical commentator Bruce J. Malina explained well this crisis of identity, describing the nature of marriage:

> The bride's family looks for a groom who will be a good provider, a kind father, and a respected citizen. The bride does not look to him for companionship or comfort. Instead . . . the new wife will not be integrated into her husband's family [until] she is the mother of a son; the birth of a son assures her security and status recognition in her husband's family.[1]

Simply put, the acceptance, value, and care Sarai longed for could be found only in producing a son for Abram. Again, this is sad on many levels, including the extreme lack of faith she displayed in taking matters into her own hands. But this story isn't about Sarai. It is about Hagar.

As challenging as Sarai's plight was, Hagar's was infinitely more desperate. For starters, Hagar was a slave. You can imagine how powerless Hagar must have felt, overhearing this conversation between Sarai and Abram but having no say in the matter. Being treated as one of Sarai's possessions to be used and abused in any way that best served the needs of her mistress. And what a poor display of faith in God Abram and Sarai demonstrated to this girl of a different nation, one of the nations promised blessing through the Israelites only a few chapters earlier. Despite her masters' portrayal of God as one who needed help fulfilling his promises, even in seedy and perverse ways, Hagar had no choice but to go along with the plan. She became Abram's wife and conceived a child.

Strangely enough (sarcasm intended), this did not improve the family dynamics. Sarai had schemed, and now a child was on the way. But Hagar began to look at Sarai with disdain. This shouldn't be too surprising, but what happened next was. When Sarai blamed Abram for Hagar's emotional state, Abram gave Hagar over to Sarai to do to her as she pleased (Gen. 16:6). Again, consider Hagar, a slave girl, with no option to choose her own spouse or decide if and when to have children. She was given over to her owner's husband for marriage. And when her new husband felt the frustration of his first wife, who faithlessly caused this entire mess in the first place, he made no move to defend the now-pregnant Hagar. He washed his hands of her. And Sarai in turn mistreated Hagar so severely that Hagar ran away.

Here is the crux of the story: when God's representatives proved unfaithful, God entered the scene. He did not leave Hagar alone in her misery. When Abram failed to protect and provide, God showed up. When Sarai pushed Hagar away, God pursued Hagar and met her just as she was—alone and broken, frightened and angry.

"Where have you come from and where are you going?" the angel of the Lord asked, finding Hagar by a spring of water in the wilderness (Gen. 16:8). I cannot help but be reminded of the garden of Eden. Remember when Adam and Eve were hiding and God asked, "Where are you?" (3:9)? Once again, we find a question being asked by a divine being.

Here's an exegetical tip to remember when studying the Bible: whenever the omniscient, omnipresent God asked someone where they were, where they were going, or where they have been, he was probably not inquiring about their location. This is similar to the time Jesus asked his disciples what they were discussing, just so they would have to say it out loud and hear how ridiculous it sounded (Mark 9:33–34). When God asked a question, it had an intended outcome.

God wanted Hagar to *consider* where she had been and where she was going. He wanted her to look at her story and acknowledge her current identity.

God Redefines Us

Hagar answered, "I am fleeing from my mistress Sarai" (Gen. 16:8). She was running away, returning to her homeland. She had good reason. Where else could she go? The Lord saw this and knew best what Hagar needed, but the instructions he was about to give were probably the last thing she wanted to hear.

The angel of the Lord said, "Return to your mistress and submit to her" (v. 9).

Stop right there. Why would a liberating God ask Hagar to return to a life of slavery? Why would the God that Scripture reveals as an advocate for his people, a deliverer of the oppressed, and Savior of the broken tell Hagar to return to her previous situation in which she was mistreated and objectified? What kind of God would ask such a thing?

Simply put, the God who sees us—and redefines us. Scripture doesn't give details about the angel's tone or demeanor, but I like to imagine he knelt close to her as she sat uncomfortably, probably in her second or third trimester, by that spring. He spoke promises over her, promises of a new identity. He told her of the multitudes she would bring to life, more than could even be counted. And this nation of offspring would come from a son named Ishmael, a name that means "God hears."

Strangely, God didn't save Hagar from the circumstances she hoped to leave. But he saw her, heard her, and promised to give her a new identity right in the midst of her old circumstances. Her liberation wasn't from the home of Sarai and Abram. And one might even say God sent her back for her own protection. He didn't remove her from the hard future she faced, but he promised her that good would come from her suffering. He promised her a legacy—scores of descendants who would not be slaves.

But the Lord's sweetest promise to Hagar was simply that she would always be seen. As lonely as she was by that spring in the wilderness, she wasn't alone. She had never spent a moment out of God's sight. Hagar exclaimed, "You are a God of seeing. . . . Truly here I have seen him who looks after me" (Gen. 16:13).

Oh, what peace must have flooded Hagar's soul as she finally felt seen and known. And not just by anyone—by the very God of the universe. After her mistress had rejected her and her husband had discarded her, Hagar was met by God in her grief, and his presence was enough. Her identity was no longer "slave girl" or "runaway" or "discarded" or "forgotten." Her identity was one who was seen and dearly loved by God.

I don't know if you identify with Hagar as I do, but let me ask you a question. Aren't you grateful we have a God who pursues us when we find ourselves in any kind of wilderness? Aren't you glad our God bends down low to speak over us? Aren't you blessed our God sees us?

I find such comfort knowing these are traits of my heavenly Father!

Identity Theft

Each year I attend fifteen to twenty women's conferences. It's actually one of my favorite parts of my job! I love meeting people, learning their names, and hearing their stories. Usually the hospitality team (or just some sweet lady in the church with good handwriting) has made name tags for each attendee. Those name tags are such a blessing. When I'm surrounded by a group of women I have never met before, it is so nice to be able to say, "Hey, Sally! I love your shirt!" Or "Hi, Linda! I've been in a car for the past four hours. Can you tell me where the bathroom is?"

As beautiful as these name tags are, I wonder what they would say if we were asked to write down our true identities. Not our *truest* identity as daughters of the King, but the identities we often take upon ourselves as though they were true.

What would you write if you were asked to fill out a name tag with one word that reflects your perceived identity? What's that part of you that you often think defines you? Maybe your word selection would be shaded by some past mistake. Maybe it would be a name you've been called by an angry spouse, a disapproving parent, or a wayward child. How many people would walk around with the label "divorced"? How many would walk around labeled "infertile"? Maybe it's not a word at all but the daily defeating number you look down and see on your scale or on the tag of your jeans. "Anxious"? "Adulterer"? "Addict"? Or maybe your label would simply say, "Not good enough."

It's possible your word isn't negative at all but rather a highlight of your life story, such as "CEO" or "Miss Teen Alabama." Even the most glamorous labels come with expectations tied to them. *What if I can't live up? If that's who I was then, who am I now?*

A few years back, a conflict arose between one of my coworkers and me. We have since worked it out, and we now work rather nicely together and can laugh about the skirmishes we had early on. It happened during a period of transition in both of our jobs. Like many job-related conflicts, this one arose when I was unable to convince all my coworkers of the sheer brilliance of an idea I had. That should have been my first clue that I was in the wrong. Anyway, a decision needed to be made, and the more I pushed for the outcome I desired, the more frustrated this coworker became with me. Finally, on a late-night phone call, I exclaimed, "Are you even listening to me?"

"Yes, Laura!" he responded. "But you're just exhausting me!"

In the moment I didn't say a single word. I went radio silent and stayed that way for weeks. I no longer engaged in meetings he attended. I no longer shared my thoughts on issues with which he was involved. I basically acted like a big ole baby whose ego had been wounded. My retaliation was the silent treatment.

That's how I responded on the outside. But on the inside? I took his offhand comment—which, honestly, was a pretty fair assessment of my behavior—and did two things with it. First, I changed it from a comment on my behavior to a description of my identity. Then I made it a label and attached it to my person, as surely as I might attach a broach to a sweater. I allowed it to move from the way someone experienced me in a particular moment on a particular topic, to a defining characteristic of my identity.

"Hi, I'm Laura, and I am exhausting."

See how easy that was? Yes, he could have chosen a kinder way to give me some much-needed feedback about how I managed stress in the workplace. But ultimately, the blame was on me. And not just for how I acted but for allowing his comment to define me.

This is the worst form of identity theft. It goes deeper than when someone steals our credit card, goes on a shopping spree, and leaves us with debts to sort out. (And if you have never experienced this form of criminal thievery, trust me when I say it's pretty awful.) When we allow ourselves to become defined by our pains or our pleasures, our failures or our achievements, we commit a crime against ourselves.

Just because you've been divorced doesn't make "divorced" your identity. It is, indeed, a part of your story, and it is likely a painful part. But in reality, it's probably a chapter in which God was given the opportunity to showcase his grace and redemptive mercy.

Just because you are struggling with an addiction that seems to control every piece of who you are doesn't mean your addiction defines you.

Just because you have fallen again to that same behavioral snare, the habit you can't quite seem to kick, doesn't disqualify you as God's child. No matter how ashamed you feel, the eyes of the Father look on you with love every single time.

You and I are not the sum of our worst mistakes or our greatest accomplishments.

You and I are not the sum of our worst mistakes or our greatest accomplishments.

Our identity is in Christ, not in our sin, our past, or our bad decisions. Not in ourselves, not in who people say we are. Not in what we think of ourselves.

Paul tells us in 2 Corinthians 5:17–19 that if we are in Christ, we are new creations. "The old has passed away; . . . the new has come." He goes on to say, "All of this is from God, who through Christ reconciled . . . the world to himself, not counting their trespasses against them." So to believe that our value is based on our behavior is to call God a liar. We must trust who Christ says we are.

A New Name

Like Hagar, our identity is found in being seen and cared for by a loving God. The name tag God made for you says "Child of the King." We are due every blessing to which that name entitles us because our identity as sons and daughters of God was purchased for us on the cross, never to be revoked.

The story that most immediately comes to mind when I speak about identity belongs to my husband. I know Martin better than anyone else, and I know he would tell you that identity is his greatest single struggle. As his wife, I see it too. But I am daily encouraged by how hard he fights to believe truth and live in the light of how God sees him.

Martin grew up playing sports and was the best athlete on any team he joined—my completely unbiased opinion, of course! Growing up he excelled at both baseball and football, gifted not only in his ability but in his work ethic. I share this with you so you can imagine how hard it must have been for someone with such talents to all of a sudden enter the world of disability. I mentioned earlier some of the ways Martin's brain injury has altered the normalcy of our lives. But Martin's deeper struggle has been one of identity.

Where many people find identity in a blossoming career and a job well done, Martin cannot. Where others find identity in their independence and self-sufficiency, Martin cannot. Martin is unable to drive and needs others to help him with rides or running errands. Don't get me wrong; Martin is extremely high functioning for a brain-injury survivor. He self-administers a litany of medications, keeps track of his doctor's appointments, and contributes daily in many ways around our home and at our church.

If you asked him how his disability has affected his sense of identity, he would tell you about his early days after surgery. He would confess his struggle of comparing his life to others', his job to the careers of those he graduated with. He would tell you, honestly and vulnerably, that he misses driving, being able to go where he wants when he wants. But despite the losses, Martin would also tell you that his previous idea of identity was attached to the wrong things.

You would hear him say that God has leveraged his disability to strip down that faulty perception of what made Martin, well, *Martin* and has given him something sturdier and much more fulfilling. You see, Martin became a Christian in college, and just like my own situation with my arm, God used a broken wrist to help him see that his value to God was based on more than his abilities. As an athlete who felt validated by the praises received from excelling, Martin endured an injury that made him unable to perform or acquire approval. He discovered he could only be loved by God because of the work of Christ.

During that season Martin learned how to live out the gospel each day, looking to Jesus rather than his talents for a sense of wholeness and identity. And that was the God-given foundation he would need for walking through disability with confident trust in those same principles.

Martin and I often remark that he's a different kind of dad than he would have been without his disability. Whenever he sees a limitation, I challenge him to see it as an opportunity. Yes, we both grieve that Martin can't drive the kids to school or remember every classmate's name. (Heck, those of us without disabilities can't even do that!) But name recognition and carpool participation aren't what make a dad great. A great father is one who loves his kids enough to kneel down and speak their identity over them every day. One who tells them they're valuable no matter how good they are at this or that. No matter how they feel about themselves or what name another kid tried to pin on them. A great dad, like our good heavenly Father, affirms his children with a truer definition of identity than this world offers.

My prayer for you is that, like Martin, you don't just affirm others with their true biblical identity. May you hear for yourself the beautiful truth of who God says you are. And may you learn to walk in it boldly every day.

So Long, Normal Story

Kevin Chung

Meet Kevin Chung

Born and raised in Georgia, Kevin Chung is a twenty-five-year-old Korean American singer and recording artist. After completing a two-year residency program at Perimeter Church, Kevin accepted a full-time position there as a worship leader.

Laura: Describe the normal you used to know.

Kevin: I grew up in a Korean Presbyterian church, the same one my parents and grandparents have always attended. I learned to lead worship there, as well as in a college ministry at University of Georgia. This was my normal, for me and for my family, as long as I can remember. My church was like a second home, where I found community and a sense of identity.

Laura: What happened in your life to bring you to the place of saying so long to normal?

Kevin: When I went off to college, it was the first time I began to view God through different lenses, not just as a Korean American. It was a huge time of growth for me. After college, I was contacted by Perimeter Church about a worship leader residency program. I didn't know much about Perimeter Church, but I knew it was predominantly white. Accepting the position required me to uproot from my community and, in a lot of ways, start over.

Laura: What was that first Sunday leading worship like?

Kevin: It was terrifying. I was looking out at a sea of white faces, the same color as the kids in elementary school who had made fun of me for how my eyes looked. I remember in middle school, in an effort to be accepted, I actually started to make fun of myself for being Asian. It was the cool thing to do, and it made the other kids laugh, which helped me to fit in better. I did what I needed to do to belong.

So that first Sunday at Perimeter, I remember thinking, *God, you are calling me to lead people, and to love people, who remind me of a scar in my past.* I was reminded of a time I didn't feel loved, of a time I had to perform or pretend in order to be accepted.

Laura: What has been your steady?

Kevin: My steady has been a sense of calling. I know now that God has called me to serve exactly where I am, whether it feels comfortable or not. And God confirmed that calling through a small note I received one day.

Toward the end of the residency, I was hanging out with a friend, wrestling with the decision of whether or not to accept a full-time position Perimeter Church had just offered me. I also had an opportunity to go back to Korea and pursue music there. Right then, a little Korean boy, maybe eight years old, came up to me and awkwardly handed me a note. I asked him his name and we talked a second; then he ran back over to his family. I opened it and began to read. It was from his mom. She was thanking me for being Korean and for being a worship leader. She continued to write that her son had always struggled with being a Korean American in a predominantly white community. When he watched movies, they always portrayed the Asian actors as the bad guys and the white male as the hero. There had been no pictures for him to look to for inspiration, no role models. But she said that my leading worship here had given him confidence. I had become that role model.

When I first got that note, I thought it was cool. But later when I shared it with my boss, he asked if he could share it in our staff meeting the following day. It wasn't until he read it aloud that the impact of those words set in, and I began to weep. We all did, but especially me. It was like God was confirming that calling and purpose in me. Since then, I've known that God has me here for a reason.

Laura: What has been your gain?

Kevin: The Lord has used this job to show me how much bias I have in my own heart. As ethnic minorities, sometimes we give ourselves too much credit. We think, *I'm woke, I'm enlightened,* but deep down, we all have prejudices. Through the friendships I've developed with people who don't look like me, who are from completely different backgrounds than me, I'm finding a new definition of identity.

Identity is not about a certain culture of this world. It's about a kingdom of another world. And the more people were affirming me for being Korean, telling me it's a beautiful thing, the more I could begin to accept my Christ-given identity as his child. Leading at Perimeter has been a big part of that journey for me. But it started with me stepping out into something that wasn't comfortable, and to something unfamiliar.

Laura: Kevin, I am so glad you took that step. And I can say this from experience: when you lead worship, you sing as someone who knows Jesus is his identity. You sing from that place of security and acceptance. I am so grateful for you, brother.

Chapter Six

So Long, Expectations

Our kids had long expressed a desire to try fishing. And when the worldwide pandemic hit in 2020, closing every school, playground, library, and Chuck E. Cheese in the country, Martin and I had to find something creative to do with them.

Fortunately my parents have a home along a beautiful coastal creek near Charleston, South Carolina. So we took each of the kids out to let them try their hand at catching fish. First, I took Josie. She started off greatly perplexed by the fact that we were going to use fish (mudminnows) to catch fish. "Can't we just eat *these* fish?" she asked. Josie spent the first part of the afternoon completely grossed out after we suggested she reach her hand in a bucket to snatch up a baitfish. "Can I run back to the house and wash my hands?"

No, I thought, *this is fishing! If you don't get fish guts all over yourself, you're not doing it right!*

After we finally got her hook baited, her hands washed, and her line cast, surprisingly she caught a fish after about twenty minutes. A nice little spottail bass, which Martin cleaned for her and we eventually ate for dinner one night. Once Josie caught a fish, the boys immediately wanted to "go get a fish too."

I tried to explain that it wasn't quite that easy, but they insisted. I took Griffin, my sweet, sensitive soul, the next day. He didn't mind getting his hands dirty and was a pretty decent caster, but I soon noticed a look of concern on his face. "Mommy, isn't this like lying?"

"What do you mean, honey?"

"Well, if the big fish thinks it is eating the little fish for dinner, but actually, *we* are eating *it* for dinner, isn't that tricking it?" This had me a bit stumped, so I let him leave due to personal conviction.

Next he sent down his brother Ben, who is more of a shoot-first, aim-later kind of guy. I knew Ben wouldn't get hung up on the moral implications of our pursuit. No, Ben instead got hung up, literally, on every other object within a ten-yard radius. He cast that mudminnow into everything but the creek, hitting it multiple times on the wooden dock, wrapping it around dock posts, dragging it across the grass, and nearly missing my head a few times. Then after a brief bit of unsuccessful casting, he asked, "Why am I not catching anything?!"

Because, Ben, the fish live in the water. The one place you have yet to land a cast!

Needless to say, we ended up ordering pizza, and everyone was happy.

As I think back to our fishing fiasco, I realized that part of the problem was my own failure to set correct expectations. Fishing is not like pulling up to Captain D's and asking for the number-three combo. Fishing can be messy, it can take a long time, and there are no promised outcomes.

Much of life's enjoyment relies on correct expectations. That's why we read all the Tripadvisor reviews before booking a trip. No fun showing up expecting the Ritz-Carlton and finding instead the

Bates Motel. If, when interviewing for a job, we ask what will be expected of us and determine what to expect from the potential employer, we'll be so much more likely to succeed.

Expectations aren't always about such clinical things. I've had many conversations with girlfriends over coffee, trying to sort out how they are feeling over some recent event. Usually when we dig down deep enough, we eventually get to this very word: *expectations*. Our expectations of marriage were too romanticized, so we ended up disappointed. The expectations we held for our children were too rigid, so we became frustrated. We expected the job of our dreams, yet found it unfulfilling. And these are only our expectations of external things.

We also battle our expectations of ourselves, and the expectations others place on us. And when we dig still deeper, we discover we're even harboring expectations of God. These can make or break our spiritual lives. When God lives up to our expectations, we thrive spiritually. When he doesn't, we are left disillusioned.

It is not wrong to have expectations. But at times along the way, we may find that saying goodbye to our normal expectations is a healthy step to take. We do this in a sense by faith, believing God has a plan that's better than even our best expectations.

Choosing Gratitude

I am not suggesting we give up on making plans or hoping for good things, but rather that we allow God to rebuild our expectations in light of who he is and what he has promised. When we place our hope and anticipation in these kinds of expectations, we can be confident they will never be destroyed.

Another girl in the Bible who entertained certain expectations of her life, love, and family was Mary, the mother of Jesus. Not only did Mary expect her life to look a certain way, but her family and community also expected her life to look a certain way. A Hebrew girl had to meet the status quo. We can be fairly sure that the life she had planned was much more normal than the one God had in mind.

Then came that one glorious night.

The book of Luke begins with the announcement of the birth of John the Baptist, a child promised to Mary's relatives Zechariah and Elizabeth. As in the situation with Abram and Sarai, God here again surprised an older, childless couple with a promised descendant who was foretold to play a prominent role in God's story of redemption. A few verses after that announcement, God surprised another woman, Mary, with a birth announcement. Yet this was a surprise for very different reasons.

For one thing, Mary was much younger than Elizabeth. Most theologians believe she was just a teenager. Also, Mary was a virgin, engaged to a man named Joseph. One of my kids' favorite Christmas movies is Sony Pictures' animated film *The Star*. Though it may not be historically accurate—the main character is a talking donkey, after all—it does a reasonably good job of showing what life may have been like for Mary and Joseph. They were a normal Hebrew couple, betrothed to one another, which was normal in their culture. They likely had a normal wedding and first year of marriage planned. Joseph had a normal job as a carpenter, probably taking over the normal family business.

But what happened next turned normal upside down.

"Greetings, O favored one, the Lord is with you!" (Luke 1:28). Imagine you're going about your normal day, preparing for your wedding, probably finishing up some invitations and discussing last-minute details with the caterer. All of a sudden, the angel Gabriel appears out of nowhere bearing greetings!

And from what we can piece together from other parts of Scripture, Gabriel probably wasn't like one of those Precious Moments figurines, a cute baby cherub floating on a cloud through Mary's window. The angels we read about in the Bible were fearsome, radiant creatures, and Mary was "greatly troubled" (v. 29). But Gabriel immediately sought to calm her. "Do not be afraid, Mary, for you have found favor with God. And behold, you will conceive in your womb and bear a son, and you shall call his name Jesus. He will be great and will be called the Son of the Most High. And the Lord God will give to him the throne of his father David, and he will reign over the house of Jacob forever, and of his kingdom there will be no end" (vv. 30–33).

To suggest that this message would have been overwhelming is probably the greatest understatement ever. If Mary had normal prewedding jitters before, this news likely sent her right over the edge! *How is it possible that I, Mary, a virgin, a simple Hebrew girl, will carry in my womb the Messiah? Am I truly to become the mother of the Creator of the universe? Are you sure you have the right girl?* These questions would have been right on the tip of my tongue. Surprisingly, Mary's response was different. She responded with submission, gratitude, and great expectation.

First, she submitted. How do we see this modeled? Mary listened to the angel, understandably asking a clarifying question or two. Then, seemingly without missing a beat, she responded in the most remarkable way: "Behold, I am the servant of the Lord; let it be to me according to your word" (v. 38). The Greek word used for "servant" here is *doule*, meaning "handmaid" or "slave girl." In the same way a handmaiden might carry out the wishes of her mistress without argument or hesitation, Mary yielded to the wishes and will of God. Mary saw herself as created by him, belonging to him, and completely allegiant to him.

It's worth noting that she responded in this manner without knowing how the story would unfold. Mary wasn't yet privy to what happened in the rest of the book of Luke. Think about her present situation. She had no assurance the angel would enlighten her betrothed, nor any insight into how Joseph would respond after hearing this most unusual news. What if no one believed her? Mosaic law dictated that the penalty for adultery, which would apply to someone betrothed, was death.[1] Mary's obedience was not simply a private heart decision. If the angel's announcement came to pass as presented, it would cost not only her but those she loved. It would cause suffering and embarrassment for her fiancé and her family. They might even be expelled from the synagogue. Yet it seems Mary responded without hesitation, but with submission. She laid down her life and her expectations before God.

Second, Mary responded with gratitude. Upon hearing the news, Mary ran to the hill country to see her cousin Elizabeth and celebrate the blessings they had both received from God. When Mary arrived, she began to sing as though she were starring in a Rodgers and Hammerstein musical:

> My soul magnifies the Lord,
> and my spirit rejoices in God my Savior,
> for he has looked on the humble estate of his servant.
> For behold, from now on all generations will call me
> blessed;
> for he who is mighty has done great things for me,
> and holy is his name. (Luke 1:46–49)

Mary's response of overwhelming joy and gratitude was genuine. Sure, she would have had moments of anxiety, of wondering how everything would work logistically. First-time expectant mothers have a right to be nervous about pregnancy—and that's especially true for someone carrying the Son of God! Whatever fears she faced, she overcame with praise. More specifically, with singing! She sang of the goodness of God. She sang of his faithfulness to generations before her and his assurance of faithfulness to the generations to come. She proclaimed the holiness of his name, trusting that there are no mistakes in his plans and no error in his ways.

Mary's song kept her heart steady as she departed from normal.

Lastly, Mary responded with great expectation. We began this chapter looking at our expectations in a somewhat negative light. Just consider the number of expectations destroyed by COVID-19. The impact has been significant. Like many couples, my brother and his fiancée had been planning their wedding for spring 2020. What was initially planned as a large celebration with friends and family from all stages of their lives ended up a small, socially distanced ceremony in our neighbors' backyard with only a handful of people in attendance. It was still beautiful and incredibly special, but when they look at their wedding photos years from now, they'll remember how it differed from what they had anticipated.

Whether it was a wedding, the normal freshman college experience you expected, or even the normal way you used to shop for groceries, chances are your expectations, too, were dashed by the pandemic.

We're used to speaking in the negative of expectations that must be lowered, plans that go unmet, and hopes being destroyed. But when we speak of Mary's expectation, we have to be amazed by such faith within her soul that God would do great things, even through the unprecedented circumstances to which he was calling her. Mary had to say goodbye to the normal engagement and marriage she had likely dreamed about since childhood. But in exchange, she was invited to be part of something beyond her wildest dreams. Rather than running from God's plan due to its abnormality, Mary was expectant! She was sitting on the edge of her seat, excited to see what God was about to do through her.

Abundantly More Than We Ask or Think

Mary's cheerful anticipation flips the script on the word *expectation*. But isn't this the kind of thing God delights in doing?

C. S. Lewis famously wrote,

> It would seem that Our Lord finds our desires not too strong, but too weak. We are half-hearted creatures, fooling about with drink and sex and ambition when infinite joy is offered us, like an ignorant child who wants to go on making mud pies in a slum because he cannot imagine what is meant by the offer of a holiday at the sea. We are far too easily pleased.[2]

I don't offer these words to minimize the emotions attached to our human expectations. It isn't wrong to long to see our children walk across a stage in cap and gown, celebrating the grand achievement of graduation, for example. It's good and necessary to make plans and natural to expect those plans to go through without a hitch. But what if our expectations are limiting the work God wants to accomplish in and through us?

What if our expectations are hindering us from being part of something God has in store that goes exceedingly beyond our hopes and dreams? If we believe God to be as Paul described him in Ephesians 3:20, "able to do far more abundantly beyond all that we ask or think, according to the power that works within us" (NASB), is it possible our expectations are too small? If we're less likely to ask God for those things that are hard to imagine happening, is it possible our expectations are limiting our prayer lives?

Commentators have long studied the Song of Mary, often referred to as the *Magnificat*. Some believe the song already existed, and Mary just sang it in that moment, kind of like when I burst into the "Hallelujah" chorus from Handel's *Messiah* (which I do routinely, if I'm having an exceptionally good day). Others believe God gave her the words in the moment, enabling her to utter the most eloquent sentiments of her heart. Yet a third possibility has been raised as well, and I truly love the picture it paints.

What if our expectations are hindering us from being part of something God has in store that goes exceedingly beyond our hopes and dreams?

Though we are told Mary hastily ran to see Elizabeth, even the fastest route would have constituted a four-day journey. Commentator Josephine Massyngbaerde Ford believes that Mary's song is likely the product of a long trek in which she had plenty of time to contemplate what was being asked of her.[3] Time to calculate the cost. Time to consider the gain, for herself and for the whole world. On such a journey, she may have grieved the altering of her engagement and marriage plans. She may have wept, pouring out her heart to God, surrendering every fear. Might she have borrowed words from David the psalmist, expressing both her doubt and her reaffirmed commitment to wait on the Lord and trust him alone?

Whatever the trip involved, and whatever those long hours alone with the Lord looked like, we can take comfort in knowing that Mary's shift in expectations was just that, a journey. As we seek to say goodbye to normal and to the expectations we hold for our lives, our families, and our futures—and all the orderly patterns we left back in Eden—we may not be ready to sing that happy song just yet. But thankfully the Lord says he will turn our "mourning into dancing" (Ps. 30:11).

Our role is to simply take the next step in front of us, asking God to turn any disappointed expectations into a greater expectation of what he will do in and through us.

Higher Hopes

Though Mary's story is inspiring, it may also feel a little discouraging. Does anyone really have such faith? What about those of us who don't typically respond with submission and praise when our dreams are dashed? If this is you, allow me to share another story—one you may relate to more.

When it came to expectations, there was probably no one more misunderstood than Jesus. Some expected nothing of him, reducing him to a bum from Nazareth, the son of a carpenter. Others expected him to become a great political figure who would fight for the Hebrews' cause against the Romans. Eventually Jesus' true mission would exceed everyone's expectations. But the scope of it was seldom recognized during the short thirty-three years he walked this earth. Even his disciples displayed misplaced expectations of Jesus.

Once, James and John approached Jesus and said, "Teacher, we want You to do for us whatever we ask of You" (Mark 10:35 NASB). It's hard not to cringe when I read those words. Really? They're speaking to their Lord, the one for whom they had left everything behind. And rather than asking what *they* could do for *him* on this day, they were asking him to grant their wishes. These guys had been following Jesus for some time now. They'd seen him do extraordinary things. For two guys who were part of his inner circle, in that moment, they sure seemed to miss the essence of discipleship.

But Jesus, rather than responding sarcastically like I would have, simply asked them, "What do you want Me to do for you?" (v. 36 NASB). Maybe he wanted them to hear the absurdity of the words coming out of their mouths. More likely, Jesus was pressing in, drawing their hearts out a bit. Jesus was known for asking questions, for digging deeper to people's root desires rather than their surface requests.

The disciples' response? "Grant us to sit, one at your right hand and one at your left, in your glory" (v. 37). On one level, James' and John's expectations were understandable. Jesus had claimed to be Lord, and he was their close friend. So why not ask Jesus for a seat next to him as he ruled? But there was a fatal flaw in their request. Their expectation of Jesus was based on *their* desires, not his. James and John were asking for two things—control and exaltation. As absurd as it may sound, I have to admit the presence of those same two desires in my own heart.

Can you relate to this desire for control? *Lord, I see how you multiply bread when people are hungry and heal the sick with just one touch. Yet I can't seem to make anything go my way! Can't I have at least one day that goes according to plan, one child who falls in line with our house rules, or even a hair day that is somewhat selfie worthy?*

How about their desire for exultation? *I know I should only care what you think of me, Lord, but it sure feels good when people "like" the picture of the healthy dinner I made. Why do I care what people think of me? What is it about me that wants others not only to accept me but to recognize, honor, and adore me as well?*

When we are honest, our desire for control and exaltation goes beyond positioning ourselves and gaining the "Most Popular" superlative our senior year. Maybe we don't want everyone to worship us, but we certainly don't mind being esteemed, admired, or applauded.

The truth is that James and John weren't too far off base in their request. Our human nature nudges all of us toward these desires to some extent. But Jesus will not become the means to their, or our, selfish ends.

Rather than blasting these guys for their self-focused expectations, Jesus, in his gentleness, painted them a truer picture of what it meant to share in what was set before him. Yes, we see a light rebuking of James and John and some chastisement by the disciples, but then Jesus shares with the larger group a fuller picture of what they should expect.

> Jesus called them to him and said to them, "You know that those who are considered rulers of the Gentiles lord it over them, and their great ones exercise authority over them. But it shall not be so among you. But whoever would be great among you must be your servant, and whoever would be first among you must be slave of all. For even the Son of Man came not to be served but to serve, and to give his life as a ransom for many." (Mark 10:42–45)

To paraphrase, Jesus told them they were right. There were plenty of religious leaders who used their power for self-exaltation, for control and superiority. But Jesus wasn't one of them. And I imagine him lowering his voice a bit and speaking the next line slowly. *It. Shall. Not. Be. So. Among. You. Rather than exaltation, my way is humility. Rather than self-assertion, my way is self-denial. Yes, you will reign with me in eternity. But first, you must become servants and slaves. If you follow me, this is what you should expect.*

I hope I haven't been too hard on these guys. As I said, I completely resonate with their self-focused desires. And if you read on, you will find that Jesus didn't ditch them and grab a new crew of disciples. He patiently bore with them, even when they left him. Even when they denied him. He forgave to the point of using them to build his church. What a beautiful picture of restoration!

To close this chapter, I want to return to the question Jesus put to James and John right before they gave their less-than-ideal answer. He asked them, "What do you want me to do for you?" On some level, his question goes beyond his initial audience. It extends to everyone who reads this exchange with his disciples. It extends to you and me.

What do you want me to do for you?

Believing that God still hears the things we ask of him and operating as if he is still the Giver of "every good and perfect gift" (James 1:17 NIV) is the basis of any thriving prayer life. How does this relate to our expectations? The late John Stott said, "The purpose of prayer is emphatically not to bend God's will to ours, but rather to align our will to his."[4]

Friend, could it be that God longs to reorient our expectations and realign our prayers according to his greater will and greater work? Could it be that dashed expectations are in fact his merciful way of saving us from lesser loves and smaller dreams?

May these words from the apostle Paul bring you comfort and godly anticipation about what lies ahead for you. This may be one of the greatest prayers of expectation ever uttered from a believer's lips:

Could it be that dashed expectations are in fact his merciful way of saving us from lesser loves and smaller dreams?

95

For this reason I bow my knees to the Father of our Lord Jesus Christ, from whom the whole family in heaven and earth is named, that He would grant you, according to the riches of His glory, to be strengthened with might through His Spirit in the inner man, that Christ may dwell in your hearts through faith; that you, being rooted and grounded in love, may be able to comprehend with all the saints what is the width and length and depth and height—to know the love of Christ which passes knowledge; that you may be filled with all the fullness of God.

Now to Him who is able to do exceedingly abundantly above all that we ask or think, according to the power that works in us, to Him be glory in the church by Christ Jesus to all generations, forever and ever. Amen. (Eph. 3:14–21 NKJV)

Is this the God you know? A God who can do "exceedingly abundantly" more than you could even think up? Be honest with him and with yourself. What is the most recent instance of disappointed expectation? It could be the cancellation of an event you **were** looking forward to or maybe something much harder, like a **job** loss, the loss of a friend, or the pain of infertility. Maybe it's even an overall disappointment, realizing you had bought into the lie that things of this world could bring more satisfaction than they actually can. Now, think back over your life. Can you remember a time when your expectations were dashed, but over time you saw that experience make way for God's better plans unfolding? And even if you haven't yet tasted of that better plan, do you ask God to give you the faith to trust him in the waiting?

Let's do it together. Let's say so long to our expectations, asking God for fresh eyes and fresh faith to expect greater things to come—greater than we could dare to dream.

Chapter Seven

So Long, Security

This past year it came time for my twin boys to begin kindergarten. I could hardly believe it! Even though I would still have little Tim at home, it was going to be a monumental change for me. Sure, I was excited, but I also knew it would be hard—on me as well as on them. So I headed to the first day of school with tissue in hand and a sweet motivational speech in mind for our tearful send-off.

As we approached the classroom door, I got down on one knee and looked straight into their beautiful eyes. "Ben and Griff, I want you to know . . ."

"See ya, Mom!" And they were gone.

I tell you this story to say this: some goodbyes are quick, and others need a bit more time. As you make your way through this book, there may be some rhythms of life or patterns of thought you can make a speedy exit from. It's like ripping off the Band-Aid: hurts a bit, but best done quickly.

But there will be other goodbyes that are more drawn out, more labor intensive, maybe even more gradual. I say this in case you feel stuck or even reluctant to leave normal. Or maybe there's something you have to say goodbye to daily, like a one-time decision to for-give that is bolstered by a thousand daily choices to live out that forgiveness.

Whatever your process or time frame for saying goodbye may be, let it be just that: *your* process, *your* time frame. God is never in a hurry, and most of his best works are long works. He is a persevering God, committed to seeing his good works through to completion (Phil. 1:6). So don't worry if these new ways of learning to let go take practice. Saying goodbye to what we're used to is always hard, but God has infinitely better things in store for you—a new season filled with new opportunities!

Of all the stories I share in this book, the story of Ruth and Naomi might be my favorite. These two women knew all too well the challenges of leaving normal behind.

In the first chapter of the book of Ruth, we find three major departures from their status quo that illuminate two very different approaches to saying so long to security. This story, which offers the best understanding of security, shows how Ruth's life was shaken in the area of provision and protection. Let's jump into it.

"In the days when the judges ruled . . ." clues us in to the context of this book of the Bible (Ruth 1:1). Ruth and Naomi lived in an odd time of civil unrest and moral chaos. Remember how God rescued the Israelites out of Egypt and guided them toward the good land he had promised? After the Israelites had wandered in the desert for forty years, God's chosen servant Joshua eventually led them to the land of Canaan. And knowing the Israelites' propensity to adopt false gods from other cultures, God instructed them to drive out the other occupants of the land. I'm pretty sure they started strong and meant to do as the Lord instructed. But eventually they found it easier to simply make their home among the Canaanites, which led to the aforementioned civil unrest and moral chaos.

With the original occupants of the land still present, war was prone to break out at any moment, making it a very unsafe time and place to live in. Moral compromise was the other by-product of living among the Canaanites. The nation that was supposed to remain pure and be a blessing to all other nations began to live no differently than any other people group. In our modern vernacular, they were "liking" the same videos on Facebook and watching *The Bachelorette* together.

See what I'm saying? The result of Israel's assimilation was at best a watered-down faith and at worst apostasy. But this wasn't the only challenge facing Ruth and Naomi in the days of the judges. "There was a famine in the land" (v. 1). You can imagine how big of a problem this was, especially in an agrarian society. People were hungry. People were broke. Times were hard.

As if things weren't bad enough, in addition to the famine, civil unrest, and moral chaos of their day, Ruth and Naomi now found themselves in a season of deep personal grief. Both women had lost their husbands. With the death of her husband, Elimelech, Naomi was left with two sons, who took for themselves Moabite wives, Orpah and Ruth. But within roughly ten years, both sons had died, and now all three women were widows. In the midst of famine, they had no husbands to provide for them. In the midst of civil unrest, they had no one to protect them. All three women faced not only the grief of losing a husband; they faced severe poverty. And for Ruth, and maybe Orpah as well, the loss of a husband prior to producing an heir added another grave loss. For these two younger women, the only hope for security was in remarrying. By the way, all this hardship is relayed in the first five verses of Ruth!

Who starts a story like this? God does. Who can take the most devastating chapter of our lives, something that may feel like a tragic ending, and turn it into the first chapter of a new and extraordinary epic?

God can.

The goal for each of these three women was to locate a new source of security. The question behind the story in the book of Ruth then is this: Where will this deep longing for provision and protection lead each of them?

Option 1: Bitterness

It's interesting to see how differently Ruth and Naomi responded to the departure of normal, and more specifically to saying goodbye to security. First, let's consider Naomi's response.

Naomi gathered her possessions and set off for Bethlehem, where she had some family. She urged her daughters-in-law to do the same: "Go, return each of you to her mother's house. May the LORD deal kindly with you, as you have dealt with the dead and with me. The LORD grant that you may find rest, each of you in the house of her husband!" (Ruth 1:8–9). Naomi bid her daughters-in-law, Ruth and Orpah, return to their Moabite relatives, to their places of origin, and to their former gods (v. 15). By not inviting her daughters-in-law to join her, Naomi was in effect saying, "Even the nicest Moabite women won't find a husband where I am going!"

Orpah relented and parted ways with Naomi as she had suggested. However, Ruth chose not to leave Naomi. We'll talk more about Ruth's response in a moment.

Naomi showed little faith in trying to send Ruth back to her family, her land, and her foreign (and forbidden) gods. Arriving in Bethlehem, she responded to the greetings of the townspeople, who recognized her, with dejection and disillusionment. "Do not call me Naomi; call me Mara [meaning *bitterness*], for the Almighty has dealt very bitterly with me." And listen to the desperation in how she described her circumstances: "I went away full, and the LORD has brought me back empty" (vv. 20, 21).

Do you find Naomi's response reminiscent of the way the Israelites misremembered their beloved normal in Egypt? I don't want to speculate too much here, but most commentators agree that Naomi and Elimelech moved to Moab believing they could find more food there, and thus a better life. So it's possible Naomi had not left Bethlehem "full," but lacking.

Isn't it interesting how we allow our memories to be reshaped to fit the narrative we want to complain about? Have you ever been guilty of rewriting a story in your mind in order to place more blame on others or on circumstances rather than on yourself? Yeah, me neither. (Just kidding.)

As if blaming our problems on others and our circumstances isn't bad enough, Naomi takes it a step further. She blames God! Don't forget the history here. Naomi was an Israelite, one of God's chosen people. Ruth was the Moabite from a land of false gods. Yet it is Naomi who was saying, *God has dealt bitterly with me.* Why was Naomi feeling so much bitterness that she changed her name to Mara?

Dean R. Ulrich sought to answer this question in his book *From Famine to Fullness.* His conclusion exposes some ugliness in my own heart:

> We often do this, do we not? We judge God's love and faithfulness by how many of our desires have been met. . . . Too often, it is not God's will that we want, but our will made possible by God. Had not Naomi made God the servant of her agenda? Do we not do the same?[1]

I don't want to beat up too badly on Naomi. She had lost a husband and two sons, and now she struggled to know where her security would come from. But what saddens me is seeing her lash out at the very one who *was* her security, the God who vowed to never leave or forsake her. Bitterness is a strong emotion, and that's the unfortunate name Naomi chose for herself. It was an unfortunate response to God's treatment. Contrast this with her daughter-in-law Ruth's faith in God's power. She wasn't a Hebrew, yet, as we will see, but she believed God to be sovereign, notwithstanding all she had endured.

In Naomi, whose heart was bitter because she failed to trust God to be good, I'm reminded that bitterness is not a by-product of a crummy set of circumstances. Bitterness is a choice we make. A place we willingly allow ourselves to go.

Be honest: How often do you allow yourself to wander into discontentment, focusing on what-ifs and why-nots? Are you actively choosing to dwell in gratitude? As Paul reminds us in Philippians 4:12, we need to learn "the secret of being content in any and every situation" (NIV).

Option 2: Faith

Ruth's response to her circumstances reminds us that two people can walk through the same situation and choose two different paths. Thankfully, Ruth did not choose bitterness like Naomi. Ruth chose faith. As a result, God was able to weave her story dynamically into the greater story of the gospel.

The loyalty she demonstrated in refusing to part ways with her mother-in-law is beautifully captured in Ruth 1:16–17, which has often been quoted during wedding ceremonies throughout the years.

Do not urge me to leave you or to return from following you. For where you go I will go, and where you lodge I will lodge. Your people shall be my people, and your God my God. Where you die I will die, and there will I be buried. May the LORD do so to me and more also if anything but death parts me from you.

Ruth wasn't interested in taking a new husband from among a people who worshipped weak and false gods. There was nothing for her back there. So she told Naomi, *I will go with you.* And in her pledge to go with her mother-in-law, Ruth wasn't looking to Naomi for provision and security. She was looking to Naomi's God. She wasn't putting her trust in Naomi for brighter days ahead. She was placing her trust in Naomi's God.

Facing the same kind of darkness, the same kind of insecurity and fear as her mother-in-law, Ruth essentially said to God, *I'd rather follow you and be single and childless all my days than to find the deepest longings of my heart met outside your will!* Ruth said goodbye to the security of the past. She cast off the temptation toward bitterness. Ruth chose faith, believing that God himself would be her security.

Ruth wasn't looking to Naomi for provision and security. She was looking to Naomi's God.

There is much more to this story, and a happy ending I highly recommend you read. You should know about the great guy Ruth meets while gleaning in his field, and the baby they have together, who ends up being the great-great-grandfather of King David, who becomes the great-great-grandfather of Jesus. (I may have left out a few *greats* in there.) When you get to chapter 4 of Ruth, your heart will be warm and joyful. But for our purposes, we will focus only on chapter 1, because most of us live in chapter 1.

The problem most of us have is not how best to celebrate the big wins of chapter 4 but how to navigate the devastating losses of chapter 1.

The book of Ruth raises a question, and I wouldn't be treating the text fairly if I didn't ask it. Here goes: In the hardest trials of your life, have you chosen the bitterness of Naomi or the faith of Ruth? In seasons of loss, have you chosen the bitterness of Naomi or the faith of Ruth? I intentionally use a form of the word *choose*. Bitterness is a feeling, but when we let it take residence in our hearts, when we allow feelings of anger toward God and unforgiveness toward others to take root, we have chosen bitterness.

I've always loved the Martin Luther adage that you cannot keep birds from flying over your head, but you can keep them from building a nest in your hair.[2] This saying highlights the distinction between merely processing our natural emotional responses, like fear, grief, disappointment, and anger, and giving ourselves over to a posture of bitterness.

Enough about bitterness. How do we choose the faith of Ruth, specifically when our security is in question? How do we choose faith when our options, like Naomi's, appear bleak? In times of great instability, when we consider the future, how do we choose faith over anxiety?

As we've noticed in previous chapters, in order to say goodbye to the things of this world, we'll have to place our full trust in the Maker of it. We can leave our homelands when we believe God is our dwelling place. We can let go of our obsession with self and the rat race of earning acceptance when we find true belonging in Christ's love. We can say goodbye to our expectations because we trust the one who can do exceedingly more than what we ask or imagine.

And, like Ruth, we can say so long to the security of our man-made plans and embrace a greater plan—a plan perfectly designed by the God who is our true provider.

Because Jesus Asks Us To

Jesus himself made a compelling plea to say so long to worldly security. On the side of a mountain, before a great crowd of people, Jesus' tender words went forth. To those he loved. To us.

> Therefore I tell you, do not be anxious about your life, what you will eat or what you will drink, nor about your body, what you will put on. Is not life more than food, and the body more than clothing? Look at the birds of the air: they neither sow nor reap nor gather into barns, and yet your heavenly Father feeds them. Are you not of more value than they? (Matt. 6:25–26)

Reading the words Jesus spoke that day, of his deep level of commitment and provision, I have to laugh. Prior to the Sermon on the Mount, Jesus' disciples had seen him turn water into wine at a wedding, transform an entire Samaritan village through his words to a thirsty woman at a well, cleanse the temple with a whip, and heal many. And prior to that, these good Hebrew boys had grown up hearing story after story of God's mighty hand—rescuing and restoring, feeding and defending, protecting his people in countless ways. By his own will God had chosen this nation as his own, for no reason other than his own delight. Why would they worry he wouldn't provide for them?

Still, living anxiety-free is not normal for most of us. Often we don't even consider worry a sin. In some settings, it's even a badge of honor. "I was up all night worrying about whether y'all would make it home okay" was something my parents often said back in my crazy band days. On one hand, we were a bunch of twenty-year-olds driving all over the country in an RV held together by duct tape and

WD-40. Our parents had every reason to worry about us! In most circles, worry tends to be synonymous with concern or care. But to Jesus' circle, on the side of that mountain, he was making it clear: worry is the antonym of faith.

Worry is wringing our hands wondering whether God will come through. Worry is a characteristic of those who don't know God or don't yet know how big he truly is. Worry is the by-product of insecurity, something God's children never have to dread, as we are always being held securely in his palm (John 10:29).

Jesus didn't speak these words in Matthew 6 to scold or condemn his children for worrying; he wanted to set them free. He was emphasizing the futility of worrying. For example, when I am anxious over unforeseen medical expenses, Jesus isn't saying, *When will you ever learn, Laura?* He isn't exasperated with my anxiety as I might be with my spouse asking me over and over again, "Are you sure you are going the right direction?" Jesus speaks words of comfort over anxiety, not condemnation. He sings over our hearts like he did to Israel through the prophet Isaiah:

Jesus speaks words of comfort over anxiety, not condemnation.

> When you pass through the waters, I will be with you;
> and through the rivers, they shall not overwhelm you;
> when you walk through fire you shall not be burned,
> and the flame shall not consume you. (Isa. 43:2)

This is God's heart toward me in my anxiety. He is constantly attentive. He is engaging the world, my world. Knowing this and believing this, I can read the next section of verses in the Sermon on the Mount and realize God has provided truth to deal with our anxiousness. Rather than obsessing about things that are often beyond my control, I can look to the one who promised he would always provide.

> Which of you by being anxious can add a single hour to his span of life? And why are you anxious about clothing? Consider the lilies of the field, how they grow: they neither toil nor spin, yet I tell you, even Solomon in all his glory was not arrayed like one of these. But if God so clothes the grass of the field, which today is alive and tomorrow is thrown into the oven, will he not much more clothe you, O you of little faith? Therefore, do not be anxious, saying, "What shall we eat?" or "What shall we drink?" or "What shall we wear?" For the Gentiles seek after all these things, and your heavenly Father knows that you need them all. But seek first the kingdom of God and his righteousness, and all these things will be added to you. (Matt. 6:27–33)

The apostle Paul had to help Timothy combat this spirit of fear and anxiousness throughout their time together in ministry. Paul encouraged Timothy with words we all should commit to memory: "God has not given us a spirit of fear, but of power and of love and of a sound mind" (2 Tim. 1:7 NKJV). God gave us his Spirit to accomplish his will throughout the world. This is not a spirit of fear; it's the Holy Spirit—a spirit of power.

When we feel fearful, we must recognize that we're allowing a spirit *other than God's Spirit* to influence us.

Whether you have heard this teaching and these verses a thousand times or this is the first time you've internalized this glorious truth, let the power of Jesus' words stop you in your tracks. Allow Jesus to step toward you. Place your hands in his. He holds the key to unshackling your wrists from the bondage of worry.

Do you hear him whispering that he takes care of every bird and every flower? Why would he neglect to provide for you, his beloved child? God already knows your every need before you even ask. You will always find him faithful.

"I Shall Not Want"

Listen, I know it is easy to be the one asking these questions. In a sense they're rhetorical. Those of us who've been around the Christian faith for any time at all can craft answers that sound good, that make us sound like we have it all together. Can I let you in on a little secret?

I struggle with feeling insecure probably more than I struggle with anything else. Despite a fairly mature faith, I still become anxious about the future. Especially when it comes to our four children and their provision, and not just financial. I struggle with whether I'll have the wisdom to be the kind of parent my kids need me to be. I get anxious about little things that could turn into big things, such as a child's allergy (*Will it grow more threatening?*) or a roof leak (*How much damage could it do to our home?*). I see a tiny bug on a windowsill and wonder, *Are unseen termites chewing up our walls? Could a wall suddenly fall off the house while we sleep?* I told you, crazy insecurity, which leads me straight to anxiety.

In light of that admission, I'll share something from Dr. Larry Crabb that really nailed me. Listen to his way-too-honest assessment of his teaching ministry:

> And there's the rub. I teach more truth than I experience, far more. The gap between what I believe and what I live raises doubts, perhaps in others about me and certainly in me about

myself and what I believe. I know the gap is supposed to breed humble, dependent faith in my heart. Sometimes it does. But even then, doubt remains, like a cloud covering the morning sun.[3]

I don't know about you, but when I read those words I immediately think, *Now there is a guy I would love to grab a cup of coffee with and have an honest conversation with about all the posing that goes on among Christians, beginning with me.* Whenever I speak or write, I am teaching the same truths I need to remind myself of daily. We never graduate. But if we keep God's truths inside our hearts, they will take us through the toughest days. I tell you this not in a theoretical sense but in a very practical I-have-lived-this sense.

I, too, need to believe what Paul said to Timothy about God's power that I have access to whenever I fear. It's a daily battle, but I'm learning. And on my best days, I recognize that the spirit of fear has no control over me. As Paul calls us to "set [our] minds on things above" (Col. 3:2 NIV), I acknowledge that my job is to choose where I set my mind. Thankfully, I have an all-powerful God I can trust with the rest.

How will we be transformed from people who are consumed with fear and anxiety to those who walk in faith, trusting completely in the one who loves us most? John Piper writes, "Transformation that comes from beholding the glory of Christ in the gospel happens incrementally. 'Beholding the glory of the Lord, [we] are being transformed into the same image from one degree of glory to another.'"[4]

I encourage you to gaze upon the finished work of Christ in the gospel, saying so long to the security this world can only pretend to offer, trusting the wealth and provision of a loving Father. As you do this, you will find yourself being transformed step by step.

I'll end this chapter with a favorite passage of Scripture that I simply want you to read. It's the psalm I often call to mind when I'm feeling insecure. Allow David's beloved words to wash over your soul and cleanse you of all anxiety and fear.

> The LORD is my shepherd; I shall not want.
>> He makes me lie down in green pastures.
> He leads me beside still waters.
>> He restores my soul.
> He leads me in paths of righteousness
>> for his name's sake.
>
> Even though I walk through the valley of the shadow of death,
>> I will fear no evil,
> for you are with me;
>> your rod and your staff,
>> they comfort me.
>
> You prepare a table before me
>> in the presence of my enemies;
> you anoint my head with oil;
>> my cup overflows.
> Surely goodness and mercy shall follow me
>> all the days of my life,
> and I shall dwell in the house of the LORD
>> forever. (Ps. 23)

A friend once shared with me that sheep without a shepherd are always looking up—looking for their next meal and staying on guard against predators. But sheep with a shepherd just graze, enjoying what's been provided for them. Do you know life in the security of the Shepherd? I pray your answer is yes. If it's not, it's time to stop trying to provide for, protect, and sustain yourself. Hear God's tender call to let go of all your doubts and fears and place your full trust in the Good Shepherd. Learn to let him lead you by the still waters. Let him restore your soul.

So Long, Normal Story

The Stack Family

Meet the Stacks

In addition to being a working mom, Tara is also the full-time caregiver for her mother, Denise, who is battling Alzheimer's disease. Tara and her husband, Davon, have been married sixteen years and have four children.

Laura: Describe the normal you used to know.
Tara: Normal looked like the typical suburban family. With three out of four kids in school, I was your typical taxicab driver, running from this activity to that. We were very busy. Our calendar was full.

Laura: What happened in your life to bring you to the place of saying so long to normal?
Tara: My mom was diagnosed with early onset Alzheimer's about four years ago, soon after my stepdad passed away from cancer. We kind of knew the diagnosis was coming, due to growing memory issues even in her late fifties. About a year later, when she began to wander, we knew we needed to move her

into memory care. Though she was doing well there, the financial strain on the family was too much. Davon and I came to the conclusion that we needed to invite her to come live with us. Our first big change was buying a new house that would accommodate her. Then we moved her in.

Laura: How has this decision affected your normal day-to-day lives?

Tara: Everything is different. Caretaking for Mom isn't only helping her get dressed and ready for the day, helping her eat, helping her swallow, and a thousand other tasks that most people can do effortlessly. Taking care of Mom is also emotionally taxing. I am her security, her safety. She doesn't know where she is most of the time. She doesn't even know that I am her daughter. She just knows I am someone who is there for her, and someone she can cling to. Our family still does a lot of what we did before, but there's now a whole new part of our lives that is caring for my mom.

Davon: Having Tara's mom come live with us has been a tremendous change. Our kids have to be conscious of how loud they are, which is hard because they are kids! Too much excitement makes Tara's mom feel jumpy, so we have to work at making our home conducive to her. We are also learning to navigate a new relationship as a couple. We aren't just caregivers for our children, but for Tara's mom now. And truly I want to honor her as Tara's mom, but there are things that can be frustrating. We're finding it's important for Tara and me to communicate well, so that taking care of her mom doesn't drive a wedge between us as a couple. Lots of evenings we take long walks in the neighborhood, just sharing how we are doing with each other, being honest about how hard things are.

It's been equally challenging for our kids, as they have had to embrace a new relationship with their grandmother. She isn't necessarily the fun-loving grandmother she used to be. She is quiet and timid now, a different person than before.

Laura: What was been your steady?

Tara: Aside from the Lord, our community has been an amazing foundation for us. This community of believers has allowed me to be the daughter God's called me to be. I will have a friend call and ask if she can just come sit with my mom while I run an errand. People bring meals, give kids rides, or just check in to see how I am doing from day to day. Caring for an elderly parent can feel so isolating. Many people don't understand the weight of what I'm walking through. And I don't always want to share how things are going, because who wants to be the downer at every dinner party? But with my close friends I can go there, and they are willing to let me not be "okay."

Laura: What has been your gain?

Davon: So many things. At the top of our list is how God has used this in the lives of our kids. There will be days when they see that Mom and Dad are at their end of ourselves, and our kids step in and ask, "Nonnie, wanna play a puzzle?" They step in and help. Our teenage boys are learning to think of others above themselves! It's changing who they are. I've even seen our oldest step into situations at school, defending someone who isn't being treated right. God is developing in him a heart to protect and care for those who cannot care for themselves.

Tara: Yeah, caring for my mom is developing in our kids such a compassion for others. Our kids are seeing what it means to serve when they don't feel like serving, and to love when they don't feel like loving. They are seeing what it means to love with endurance, to answer yes to God when it's hard. And my kids are also learning repentance . . . from the amount of times I mess up! With all the stress I'm under, I don't always love them well, or Davon, or my mom. I am often apologizing, and they see all of it! So often parents want to protect their kids from seeing their imperfections, but I think it's good to keep it real. This is how our kids learn what grace really is.

Becoming the full-time caregiver for my mom has been harder than I ever imagined, but it has brought me closer to God than I've ever been. I have been a Christian most of my life, even went to Bible college, but I am growing more now in my faith than I ever have. I am believing more and more in his goodness and his sovereignty, even when our situation doesn't *feel* good. Yes, I still pray that the Lord would change our circumstances, would bring healing, but I am also praying that as I walk through the trials, I would develop a deeper relationship with Christ. I want to know him more intimately, feel more deeply how loved I am by him.

I've gone from being a lukewarm suburban Christian to someone who craves to walk closely with the Lord, someone who desperately needs him each day. That's truly been my gain, and that makes every bit of it worth it.

Part Three

Saying Hello

I know the plans I have for you, declares
the LORD, plans for welfare and not for
evil, to give you a future and a hope.

—JEREMIAH 29:11

Chapter Eight

Hello, New Life

After a lifetime spent in South Carolina, and one year of marriage, I was uprooting, making the move with my husband to the big city of Atlanta. Or at least to the suburb of Johns Creek. I called around and priced rental trucks, even though I was slightly terrified at the thought of us driving something so monstrous. We said goodbye to all our friends and family, enjoying last dinners and coffee dates.

I know what you're thinking. *Doesn't South Carolina share a state line with Georgia? It's not as though you were moving halfway around the world.* Okay, yes. We were only moving about 150 miles down the road, but there was something so final about leaving all the places where we had spent our entire lives.

With a last omelet at Papa Sam's, the breakfast spot Martin and I had gone to every Friday morning since high school, we waved goodbye to Spartanburg and set off for our next adventure. A new life awaited us in Johns Creek, and we were giddy with excitement over this next chapter of our lives—because, whether God is telling us to stay where we are or to move into a new chapter that he may be writing in our lives, he is always at work.

For those times when we step forward into new beginnings, here's fair warning: when we yield to his will, on some level, God is calling us to leave the comfort of the familiar.

Consider my decision to step from the zip-line platform. I was choosing to step from a sturdy, well-tested structure into literal thin air for the sake of a thrilling adventure. In the same way, the spiritual adventure I'm speaking of may contain few plateaus, leading us instead on rigorous treks filled with highs and lows or the heart-sinking dip of waiting for the rope to catch. But it's a call to step out, to leave behind earthly contentment for true fulfillment and a solidarity with God that only comes from the shaking of what can be shaken.

Fair warning: when we yield to his will, on some level, God is calling us to leave the comfort of the familiar.

God never shakes us to disorient us but to *reorient* us. His sovereign shaking of our lives is a sweet mercy, freeing us from our tendency to settle for lesser joys and cheaper treasures.

Paul David Tripp said,

How can you and I not be grateful for God's patience with us? He doesn't demand of us instant maturity. He doesn't require that we get it right quickly. He doesn't teach us a lesson just once. He comes to us in situation after situation, each controlled by his sovereign grace, each designed to be a tool of transformation, and he works on the same things again and again. . . . It is his tender willingness to wait that allows his powerful grace to finish its transforming work.[1]

God loves us too much to let us settle for normal. He rescued us from the domain of darkness not just to give us life but abundant life!

So what does this abundant life look like? Time-shares in Tahiti? A thousand new Facebook friends or Instagram followers? Probably not that. What makes the abundant life Jesus offers great is that it is nothing like the "good life" the world offers.

Rather than accumulating things, this abundant life involves emptying ourselves. Rather than achieving prominent positions, the abundant life requires the posture of a servant. Rather than striving for accolades that promise a sense of significance, we are warned against seeking such notoriety. The abundant life requires bending down low. Which raises an obvious question.

What's so great about the abundant life? If we were to cast away every normal thing that comforts and validates us, what could possibly make this new life desirable and enjoyable?

As we investigate God's Word more deeply, we will better understand this new definition of the good life. We'll also discover that the abundant life we have in Christ is not only more fulfilling than anything in this world; it is the only way to find lasting fulfillment.

It's the Climb

Martin and I once hiked in the Cohutta Wilderness a couple of hours north of where we lived in Georgia. A few miles in, being fairly new to long-distance hiking, we realized that we were completely unprepared to complete the eight-mile trail we had set out to conquer. About that time our trail crossed a paved road, so we flagged down a car and got a ride back to where we parked. We wouldn't normally hitchhike, but we were pretty sure we would die of dehydration if we stayed on the trail. Hopping in a car with a stranger seemed like the lesser of two dire outcomes.

Of all the hiking stories I've told, this is my first time telling this one, and for good reason. It's a story of us copping out. We didn't finish well. We set out on a trail to see something glorious, to achieve something great. Feeling scared and unprepared, we didn't finish. We forfeited the gain we had initially sought.

The other day we set out on a fairly strenuous uphill climb with the kids. After a while, Ben, one of our twins, asked, "Mom, are there any hikes in your hike book that go downhill to get to the top of the mountain?" It was a sweet question, and it gave us all a good laugh. But the answer was no, both in hiking and in life.

This new way of life God invites us to take may be a long, hard road, a strenuous climb with an overgrown, muddy trail. But at least we can rest assured he has given us everything we need to make the journey.

The Abundant Life Will Not Be Free of Trials

Life with Christ will not be pain-free. This is a prominent theme throughout Scripture. First, let's just acknowledge how abnormal it is to embrace such a life.

When traveling from point A to point B, we enter the destination into our navigation system, expecting it will provide us with the shortest route. The one with the least amount of traffic and road construction. When we are moving toward something positive—adopting a child, for example—we pray against obstacles and roadblocks. And this is a reasonable request. But following Jesus may mean laying aside our obsession with productivity, efficiency, and timeliness. As we wind our way through each detour and trial, the lessons learned may be more valuable to God's heart than the outcome ever was.

As much as it pains me to quote Miley Cyrus, she kind of had it right. "Ain't about how fast I get there / Ain't about what's waiting on the other side / It's the climb."[2]

Along with Miley, someone else knew this well and wrote about it. In his letter to the Romans, the apostle Paul encouraged the Christians in light of the trials and tribulations they were facing. The church during this time was experiencing mistreatment at the hands of the Roman government, and storm clouds on the horizon signaled this would soon become full-scale persecution when Nero became emperor. Paul's teaching for Christians in Rome is as relevant today as it was when he wrote these words:

> Therefore, since we have been justified by faith, we have peace with God through our Lord Jesus Christ. Through him we have also obtained access by faith into this grace in which we stand, and we rejoice in hope of the glory of God. Not only that, but we rejoice in our sufferings, knowing that suffering produces endurance, and endurance produces character, and character produces hope, and hope does not put us to shame, because God's love has been poured into our hearts through the Holy Spirit who has been given to us. (Rom. 5:1–5)

Notice from the outset that Paul is not telling us the secret to living a trouble-free life, or how to avoid trouble when we see it coming. He is addressing the attitude we should adopt in the midst of suffering.

My normal response to anything hard is to figure out how to get out of it. Is there an easier way to fix the leaky shower than ripping up the entire tile floor? Must I really apologize to that person I offended? God of mercy and grace, do I *really* have to go to jury duty? While we're focused on finding the way around a trial, God is more concerned with how we live by faith *through* it.

He knows what's at stake, how the struggle can make our character more like Christ's.

Our Trials Are a Means to an End

As we continue to read the opening verses of Romans 5, we sense it is building to a climactic conclusion. And it is. Paul wrote to remind us of the joy we can now experience, the access we have to God, and the hope we have received through faith. But we quickly learn that our hope is the result of a process of endurance.

It's as if we're watching *The Price Is Right*, and we've made it all the way to the grand Showcase Showdown. Drew Carey is listing off all the wonderful items in the showcase: the new surround-sound entertainment system, the new washer-and-dryer combo, and a pair of matching Jet Skis. But then, as the excitement mounts to the grand prize, which is almost always "a *brand new car!*" the host instead announces, "Your grand prize is a month of cleaning restrooms at the rest stops along the interstate of your choice!" I say this tongue in cheek, of course. Sure, it is amazing to think about what God has for us through Christ, but Paul made it sound as though the capstone, the grand prize of the Christian life, is embracing tribulations!

But God is not the author of evil, nor is he a masochistic deity who delights in the suffering of his children. What Paul was describing here is the hard road God sometimes allows his children to walk because it is the only way to become what God created us to become. This journey is the means to producing Christ's character in us. And so Paul tells us, "We rejoice in our sufferings," not because we are crazy. Not because we have a sadistic martyr complex. Paul said it's because "suffering produces endurance, and endurance produces character, and character produces hope" (Rom. 5:3–4). Let's consider, briefly, those four words—*suffering*, *endurance*, *character*, and *hope*—and how this progression works.

First, suffering. I can almost see your faces sour at the mere mention of the word! Imagine what the word *suffering* would look like in calligraphy on a nicely distressed panel of wood. We see a thousand options for wall decor on Etsy, lovely sentiments to hang in our kitchens that say "blessed" or "grateful" or "gather." I've yet to find one of those pretty signs that says "suffering"! Yet there it is at the top of Paul's list. The very thing all of us spend an enormous amount of time and money trying to avoid is what Paul tells us leads to some of the most sought-after attributes.

Paul continued to say that suffering leads to endurance. Wait a minute. Was Paul saying that suffering always leads to endurance? Of course not. Yet you have to admit that endurance is not something you can gain without suffering. There is no longed-for finish line without the race. There is no remission to celebrate without the initial cancer. Though no one longs to suffer, it is essential to gaining the virtue of endurance. And I would even suggest, as Paul did here, that endurance is the natural by-product of suffering for the life of a Christ follower.

Not only do we gain endurance; we gain character. It's hard to imagine anyone in their right mind not wanting to be described as a person of character. But when Paul used the word our English Bibles translate as "character," he wasn't referring to someone with nary an overdue library book or unpaid parking ticket. In the Greek, the word Paul used was *dokime*, meaning "the result of trial." The version of character Paul was referring to is not possible apart from suffering. It's the diamond formed from continued exposure to the heat and pressure of the earth. It's the beautiful canyon forged by the piercing pressure of roaring waters. Character is not cheap to come by, but it may be your most valuable possession. This is the character of which Paul spoke.

Lastly, Paul shows us the product of the first three words—hope. The simple mention of the word lightens my heart. Hope is what keeps us going in the dark. It's believing that God is working in the unseen. Hope is essential to our Christian faith, but, as Paul reminds us, the faint of heart don't acquire it. It all begins with a willingness to endure suffering. Even endurance and character are not the simple by-products of attending a weekly Bible study or memorizing a favorite verse. They are works of the Spirit, birthed in our hearts along the road of suffering. In order to live lives of hope, Paul tells us we must be willing to suffer, thus practicing endurance, thus gaining character.

It's sometimes easier to see this principle playing out in others rather than in myself. For the past two years I've had the privilege of leading a small group of women in a Bible study at our church. I use the word *lead* loosely. I tell the ladies when we are meeting, we all bring our Bibles, and God teaches us through one another's insights. I would say the greatest joy of being in this group has been getting a front-row-seat view into their lives. I know by now that it is not my job to change anyone or make them "better Christians." Some of my Christian sisters have carried burdens I wish I could have taken away, but it is not my job to help them wiggle out of the hard places in their lives. I have wept with them over the loss of loved ones, the struggles in their marriages, job transitions, the processing of childhood abuse, and the pain that comes with raising children.

In the moment, I wished I could have snapped my fingers and made the pain disappear. But now, when I step back, I'm grateful I could not. Now when I look at this group of ladies, I see stronger mothers. I see a depth of dependence on the Lord that wasn't there before. I witness a gentleness of spirit where there was once anger. I see a willingness to laugh at chaos where there was once rigidity and control. I see the Lord doing so much in their lives! When I desperately wanted to pluck them out of the hard spot, God had me simply pray. In some moments, I got to crawl right in there with them. But it was God working in their trials, not my skillful teaching or fancy curriculum, that produced the fruit.

So back to Ben's question, which I'll tweak to better reflect our journey: Can we get to the amazing vista of spiritual maturity apart from the rugged climb? Paul's answer is pretty clear. But rather than this truth leading to discouragement as it did for Ben, let it bring you comfort. Just because you are walking a difficult path doesn't mean that you are on the wrong road. And in the kingdom of God, nothing is wasted.

What trial are you facing right now? Do you believe God the Father has sovereignly allowed it in your life for your good and his greater glory? Do you believe there is a specific work of sanctification, a refining of the self, that the Spirit is doing, making you into the person God wants you to be? And do you believe that obedience by grace is possible even in the hardest of trials and loneliest of seasons? The Trinity is working in you and for you. Which leads us to our next glorious truth: though our trials may be long, we are never left alone in them.

It's a Tethered Life

Though the life Jesus calls us to is a life with trials, we are never left untethered. Remember when I found myself suspended from a zip line? With no ground beneath my feet, it felt like I was careening to my death, especially in those first few moments. I was in a free fall, with nothing to grab hold of to steady myself except a single rope tied to a single line, suspended from giant trees. It was terrifying. But I was tethered.

In the same way, our new abundant life with Christ will not be free of trials, but we will not be tumbling with nothing to grab on to. We are always tethered to a great and mighty God!

When we speak of connectedness to God, we find two aspects to consider. In one sense, we are always and forever connected to God through Christ. Jesus mentioned this truth himself: "My sheep hear my voice, and I know them, and they follow me. I give them eternal life, and they will never perish, and no one will snatch them out of my hand" (John 10:27–28).

What a beautiful picture of grace! We could never commit a sin so grave that it would revoke what Christ has done on our behalf on the cross. Our place in God's family is sealed. We are forever his children. End of discussion.

But later, Jesus taught on the importance of *staying connected* with the Father. Yes, we are connected to God through Jesus, *and* we are called to stay connected by making daily, volitional choices to abide in him. Jesus chose the metaphor of plant life.

I am the true vine, and my Father is the vinedresser. Every branch in me that does not bear fruit he takes away, and every branch that does bear fruit he prunes, that it may bear more fruit. Already you are clean because of the word that I have spoken to you. Abide in me, and I in you. As the branch cannot bear fruit by itself, unless it abides in the vine, neither can you, unless you abide in me. I am the vine; you are the branches. Whoever abides in me and I in him, he it is that bears much fruit, for apart from me you can do nothing. (John 15:1–5)

For the Fruit

Here are just a few observations from this passage regarding the new life that comes from being tethered to God. First, as in any analogy, we must identify who is who in the illustration. In this case, Jesus identified himself as the vine, his Father as the vinedresser, and the disciples as the branches. This had implications for the Hebrew listeners, who assumed their connection to God was a birthright, based on their ancestry. Here, Jesus brought to light several issues simultaneously, but we'll focus on what he had to say about the necessity of abiding.

He called us to abide in him and assured us of his abiding in us. This is the positive aspect of abiding. He also gave us the negative results if we don't abide in him. He said we cannot bear fruit on our own. Imagine a fruitless life, like a tree that's been toppled by a storm, roots unearthed and unable to access nutrients from the soil. These verses paint this picture and give the definitive warning, "Apart from me you can do nothing" (John 15:5).

I've always loved the way South African writer Andrew Murray described this connectedness in his book *Abide in Christ*. In case we should misunderstand and think that abiding is a strenuous work we must do, let his words correct this flawed thinking. "It is not the doing of some great thing," Murray explained, describing what it means to abide, "and does not demand that we first lead a holy and devoted life. No, it is simply *weakness entrusting itself to a Mighty One* to be kept—the unfaithful one casting self on One who is altogether trustworthy and true."[3]

And to bring this glorious point home, Murray simplified the idea with one last thought:

Abiding in Him is not a work that we have to do as the condition for enjoying His salvation, but a consenting to let Him do all for us, and in us, and through us. [Abiding] is a work He does for us: the fruit and the power of His redeeming love. Our part is simply to yield, to trust, and to wait for what He has engaged to perform.[4]

In a chapter that has focused on the intense climb, these words remind us of the simplicity of our role: to yield. To trust. To wait. Have you come to the end of yourself? According to Murray, that's a great place to see God doing an extraordinary work through you.

For the Flourishing

It's through our yielding and trusting and waiting that we flourish. Have you ever thought of abiding this way? Or did you grow up believing a version of Christianity that relied on your efforts to do good things or simply be a good person? If this is you, look again at Murray's words and let them minister to your weary soul like a balm.

Friend, Jesus doesn't call you to *earn* his favor but to *abide* in his favor. We grow in Christlikeness when we yield to the work the Spirit is doing in and through us. The believer who wants to know true spiritual rest must learn to abide. We are not saved from hell, then patted on the back to go live a great life in our own strength. We are not given the Ten Commandments as standards we must live up to by relying on our own gumption. We are given the Holy Spirit and all the help we need to thrive.

To think of God as the vinedresser is to compare him to a caring gardener who plants and cultivates his crops. Not only does he tend to us for our flourishing, but he is also the very life force that brings about that flourishing. When we abide in God through Christ, his life flows through us and produces fruit. What joy to be merely a branch on such a vine!

Jesus went on to relate to his disciples the reason for sharing with them this secret of new life: "These things I have spoken to you, that my joy may be in you, and that your joy may be full" (John 15:11). Take a moment to really ponder this truth. Not only spiritual rest but soul-satisfying joy come from abiding in Christ!

Theoretically, we all would probably say we believe this to be true. In children's choir I sang, "I've got the joy, joy, joy, joy, down in my heart. Where?"[5] from an early age. So on some level, I've always known that my joy was found in abiding in Jesus and his abiding in me. But somewhere around middle school I began to doubt it. I figured if God would forbid me from dating Bobby Jo just because he wasn't a Christian, he must not want me to have much joy, joy, joy, joy down in my heart. And if I couldn't go to the same parties everyone else went to, he must not want me to have any fun. A seed was being planted in my mind that maybe Jesus came not to give me joy but to steal it.

Now if you read those words slowly and carefully, you'll notice they sound eerily like the conversation between the serpent and Adam and Eve. God was holding out on me! There were mysterious pleasures he didn't want me to have or experience.

Hmm. Once again, we are back in the garden.

If you happen to be a teenager reading this, you may be in exactly this position. If you are an adult, your joy imposters will probably look different. *If only I had the right house in the right neighborhood with the right two-car garage to pull my right Escalade into. Then I would be happier, which would make our kids better behaved, we'd have more friends, and I, too, could post pictures of us with important people, laughing on our back deck as we barbecue an expensive cut of meat.* Let's face it. When we choose to abide in Jesus, we have to say goodbye to many of the other places we've been abiding.

Here is the truth about those other sources of joy: they are "broken cisterns" (Jer. 2:13). The prophet Jeremiah pointed this out when the Israelites made the same kind of error. We are no different. When we look to things of this world for refreshment rather than to the Living Water God offers, we'll only sip up the last dirty dregs of stagnant water and wonder why we're still thirsty. Yes, we'll have to say our goodbyes to lesser joys. But whatever sorrows those goodbyes bring are fleeting in light of the kind of flourishing Jesus offers. He offers a *full* joy, and a filling joy. The new life we have in God may be one of trials, but we will never face those trials alone. We are tethered to a faithful God who helps us to not only survive but thrive.

> *We are tethered to a faithful God who helps us to not only survive but thrive.*

It's a Tremendous Life

When we yield to a new life in Christ and stay tethered to him even in the midst of trials, we exchange a normal life for a tremendous life. Here's how the *Merriam-Webster* online dictionary defines *tremendous*: "notable by reason of extreme size, power, greatness, or excellence." You may find synonyms like *excitement, trepidation, fear and awe, thrilling and terrifying all at the same time.* This is the Christian life—all of this!

Do you believe God calls you to an extraordinarily excellent, intense, and exciting life, which may also at times be terrifying? When we say goodbye to normal, we embark on an adventure with God that is by no means safe or predictable. We begin an extraordinary journey of faith.

God gives us the joy of Paul, who bellowed out glorious hymns while chained in a dark, dank jail cell. God gives us the endurance of Joseph, who trusted and obeyed him through every unforeseen twist and turn of his story. God gives us the audacious faith of Noah, who built a massive boat when there wasn't a single rain cloud in the sky. And God gives us the boldness of David, who danced half-naked and unashamed, celebrating the presence of his God. (Okay, maybe I'd better not encourage you to follow his example verbatim.)

The life we gain in Christ is a tremendous life. But it begins quietly, inside each of our hearts.

A Missional Heart and a Bold Faith

As I shared earlier in chapter 5, during my freshman year of college I was suffering a crisis of identity. Then seemingly out of the blue came an opportunity to travel to Mongolia with a mission organization for the purpose of sharing the good news of the gospel with the nomads who were grazing their livestock across the plains. This was my mission, something meaningful being accomplished *through me* by God's grace. But also during this mission, God began doing something *in me*.

It was on this mission, as I sat on the hillsides, gazing out on those vast plains, that everything changed for me. God stirred within me a longing to engage intentionally in the work that would become my calling, my mission, and his commission. God brought clarity to me on this trip that up until that time I had never known. Now, I'm not saying I was given a vision of future events. I had no clue about the wonders and challenges that awaited me on my journey of faith and mission. In fact, had I known, I might very well have been reluctant to embrace the call. But what I did have was a settled spirit within me.

Something was different on the inside.

Maybe for the first time, I understood in a meaningful way that God did indeed have a plan for my life. Sure, a version of his calling and his commission is given to each of us. But beyond that, there was a unique role I was to play in the story of redemption that began unfolding in the garden of Eden.

At the time, I didn't know what would come of it. I just knew God had imparted to me a heart for his mission in the world, and I would never be the same.

These days, Josie constantly brings home books about every subject under the sun, thanks to a new reading program at school. We've read about everything from photosynthesis and butterfly metamorphosis to the New Deal and the California gold rush. A few weeks ago, she presented us with a book about George Müller.[6] Now here was a man with a tremendous life.

Müller lived in nineteenth-century England and sought to be a missionary abroad when his health began to fail him. Though he initially struggled with that door closing, God opened his eyes to the great need all around him. Every day when he walked the streets of Bristol, he passed hungry children begging for just a few coins. Their cries were nearly muted because poverty was so common-place in that day and age. Yet one day, while hundreds of others kept going, Müller stopped. He *saw* that one child. Then he looked around and saw dozens of children—poor, starving, orphaned. He recognized God's image in those small faces and heard the call: God's care is shown through God's people.

Müller began by opening one orphanage, getting a handful of young children off the streets, providing them with a meal and a warm bed. He also began to teach these children, in a day and age when education was typically reserved for higher-society families.

As he raised funds for his efforts, he was often opposed and accused of trying to elevate the poor above their natural given social class. Müller's response? "It ill becomes the servant to seek to be rich, and great, and honoured in that world, where his Lord was poor, and mean, and despised."[7] Over his lifetime, Müller built 117 schools and cared for more than ten thousand orphans.

There are two things that really stood out to me when I consider George Müller's tremendous life. First, his tremendous life wasn't a result of him going but of him *staying*. Müller didn't embark on an epic journey to an exotic place. God simply gave him eyes to see the need right in front of him, in his own neighborhood.

Second, his tremendous life was a by-product of his extraordinary faith. My favorite story from Müller's life may be familiar to you. If so, try to hear it with fresh ears. Several years into Müller's mission, he sat down with three hundred orphans who were ready to eat their meal for the day. The tables were set with plates, forks, spoons, and cups. But there was one thing missing: the food. Müller had spent his very last shilling, and he truly had no idea where their next meal would come from. This, however, didn't stop him from blessing the food that he firmly believed God would provide.

"Dear Father," he began, "we thank Thee for what Thou art going to give us to eat."[8] As the story goes, at that moment a baker came knocking at the door. He said he had been unable to sleep and had a strong sense around 2:00 a.m. that Müller's orphans would need bread that day. No sooner had Müller distributed the bread to a dining room full of hungry children, but there came another knock at the door. The milkman's truck had broken down right in front of the orphanage, and there was no way to salvage the truck's full load of milk. Was there anyone at the orphanage who could maybe help drink it?

I tell you this amazing story to encourage your faith, but it's more than just that. I want you to know what happened to my children as we read the story together. Now keep in mind that I was reading this to an eight-year-old and twin six-year-olds who usually get fired up by shows about robot trains and the exciting journeys of animated rescue dogs. Yet as I told them Müller's story, their eyes got wider and wider. They were captivated. This was one of the most thrilling and amazing stories they had ever heard!

And upon closing the book, Josie said, rather emphatically, "I want to do that!"

"Do what?" I asked.

Her eyes were wide with exhilaration. "I want to see God do something big like that!"

I just grinned, quietly praying on the inside. *God, would you do this for Josie? And for Benjamin? And for Griffin and Timothy? May you grant them the faith to live boldly, to ask audaciously, and see you do extraordinary things. Grant my kids tremendous lives for your kingdom and your glory!*

I pray the same for you and me. We will face trials, but as we abide in Christ, living the tethered life of a child of God, the potential of our lives is boundless.

So Long, Normal Story

Bailey Moody

Meet Bailey Moody

A student at the University of Alabama, Bailey Moody is a childhood cancer survivor. Bailey is currently the youngest player on the U.S. Women's Wheelchair Basketball Senior National Team.

Laura: Describe the normal you used to know.
Bailey: I was diagnosed with cancer when I was ten, so there wasn't much time that anything *was* normal. I was an active kid. I was a bit of a tomboy, playing basketball and tennis, participating in jump-rope clubs, and joining any rec leagues I could find. I would go to school, then come home and play sports. That was me as a kid.

Laura: What brought you to the place of saying so long to normal?
Bailey: It started with severe pain in my right knee that was causing me trouble in sports. My parents took me in for an X-ray and an MRI, which led to the diagnosis of osteosarcoma, a rare form of bone cancer. From that moment on, my normal was gone. Everything changed. Within days of that diagnosis, I started

chemotherapy. I would go into the hospital almost every weekend for chemo and stay for five days at a time for treatment.

I lost all my hair, threw up hundreds of times, and was completely fatigued and unable to do anything. I had mouth sores that were so bad they required morphine. And a ton of other things that a normal ten-year-old kid would never deal with. I wanted to be at school with my friends and playing sports, but instead I was lying in a hospital bed.

Laura: Would you say, then, that nothing about your life was normal?
Bailey: I was ten years old, and my closest friends were nurses and hospital staff. There's nothing normal about that.

Laura: What happened next?
Bailey: My protocol for treatment was ten weeks of chemo, then surgery, then twenty more weeks of chemo. With childhood cancer, they treat it pretty aggressively since they don't know if there is cancer in other areas they can't see. Out of the three surgical options they gave us, we chose rotationplasty, which is where the bottom of the femur, the knee, and the upper tibia are surgically removed, then the lower leg is rotated 180 degrees and attached to the femur. It doesn't look normal at all, but that's what I chose because I wanted function over looks. A lot of people told me that girls should always chose looks over function. But I chose function. I wanted to play sports again, hike, swim in the ocean, jump on a trampoline, and so many other things! I knew rotationplasty would give me more of a chance of doing those things.

Laura: Once you got home from the hospital, how was life different?
Bailey: Living as an amputee is hard. People may think I make it look easy, but it's because I work hard at it, and I have high

expectations of myself. It's a lot of work behind the scenes. I've had years of physical therapy to get me to run again and keep up with my friends. I go all the time to my prosthetist, just for small tweaks, trying to get my leg exactly like I need it. Doctor's appointments became my everyday life.

Laura: How did your normal look different from normal for other middle-school students?

Bailey: I definitely felt like I grew up really fast. There is a maturity level that comes from just going through hard things, so there were times I'd hear about a friend's problem with a boy or a bad haircut, and think, *Are you kidding me?* Transitioning back to school was hard too. But once I began to share the new complexities of my life with my friends, they began to understand what I had gone through. Honestly, I was just happy to get back to my friends and for them to treat me how they had treated me before. My cancer showed me how important relationships really are.

Laura: What has been your steady?

Bailey: My steady has been remembering that God is in control, especially in situations in which I feel completely out of control. Like a lot of people, I have this terrible tendency to try to control my circumstances. Time and time again, I hear God saying, *Hold on, Bailey. I've got this.* I remember one moment, toward the end of my chemo, when I was headed to the car after treatment and began to experience stroke-like symptoms. Mentally, I was there but unable to communicate with anyone. The words just wouldn't come out. As they brought me back in and frantically tried to figure out what was going on, I was only able to talk to God. And in my desperation, I remember this overwhelming peace coming over me. He was the only person I could talk to, and he was also the only person who could truly calm me. It was like he was saying once again, *I've got this, Bailey.* I will never forget that moment.

Laura: What has been your gain?

Bailey: There have definitely been gains. My life is what it is today because of what I've walked through. I have opportunities now that I would not have had if I had not lost my leg. For instance, sports. With a lot of hard work, I was able to return to basketball only months after I finished chemo. I was back at it, but I was much slower than the other players. I could still make it down the court, but clearly people with two legs are going to be faster than people with one. That's when I started playing wheelchair basketball. I tried it and really enjoyed it. I could be fast, and the playing field was level.

After a few years, I went to a national team development camp and was asked to try out for Team USA 2018 for the world championship. With lots of hard work, I made the team and went on to play for that championship in Hamburg, Germany. The next year I made both the under-twenty-five women's national team and the senior national team. The under-twenty-five team won gold at the world championships in Suphan Buri, Thailand, and our senior team won a silver medal in the Parapan American Games in Lima, Peru. Then, at the beginning of 2020, I made the team that was supposed to go to the Paralympic Games in Tokyo, Japan!

Laura: Which, unfortunately, has been postponed due to COVID-19.

Bailey: That's right. But I'm looking forward to Tokyo 2021!

Laura: And you are the youngest player on that team! Bailey, what an amazing story. Last question: What would you say to a kid out there who, as a cancer survivor or as an amputee, feels like life has passed them by and is considering giving up?

Bailey: I would tell them this: good things *can* come from really bad circumstances. There is still light at the end of the tunnel, and God is working *all things* together for good. There are opportunities that will come from your hardship that you wouldn't have had before. What I do now, I couldn't have done with two legs. I just couldn't have.

A few years after my surgery, I got the chance to go on a mission trip to Uganda for a sports camp. It was funny because a lot of times when Americans visit an underdeveloped country, the people there have this picture that our lives are perfect. They think nothing ever goes wrong for us, and we never face anything hard. I had an opportunity to share my story with these Ugandan kids. I told them about how hard cancer was, how hard it is doing life with one leg. More importantly, I told them how I made it through. I think it was good for them to hear that everybody faces hard stuff, but when we put our faith in God, he does good things in us and through us. Things like cancer and amputations don't have to be endings. They can be new beginnings.

Chapter Nine

Hello, New Vision

You need to meet my husband, Martin, because the story I am about to tell you is really his to tell—but also because his storytelling is hilarious. Anyone who knows him knows that it's not just the stories themselves that are funny but his inability to tell a story without laughing so hard in the middle of it that he can't actually finish it!

Martin played college baseball and was really good at it, and not just by my non-sports-understanding standards. After college he continued to enjoy both watching and playing the sport whenever he had the chance. I have mentioned before that Martin has a vision deficit. Due to his brain tumor and surgery, he has irreparable damage to his optic nerve that has given him limited peripheral vision as well as double vision. It's a very serious condition, but in typical Martin fashion, he chooses to find the humor in his limitations.

A few years after the surgery, Martin became discontent just sitting on the couch rooting for the Atlanta Braves. He also met a friend at our church who, after hearing about Martin's background, invited Martin to come help him coach a travel league his son had just joined. On his first day back, all the mechanics of playing the sport were still intact, but he had underestimated how much his double vision would hinder him.

His first time on the field was with a bunch of middle schoolers. When Martin threw a ball to them, he was dead-on. But when they threw it back, he saw multiple balls flying toward him, which caused him to scream and duck. He laughs about it now, but at the time he was mortified at how unprofessional it appeared for the coach to duck every time someone tried to throw him the ball!

A couple of years later he found a doctor who was able to construct some glasses that were specifically made for his particular vision deficit. They have helped him immensely. In fact, the first time he put them on he said to me, "There's only one of you!" (I knew this would improve our marriage considerably, since I have no doubt that one of me is more than enough to handle.)

Have you ever experienced something like reading a book, visiting a memorial, or viewing a documentary that caused you to see all of life differently? It's like watching one of those independent films that explore how sausage is made. You never, ever want to eat pork products for the rest of your life—or at least the next year. Maybe you see an enormous landfill and commit to recycling and being a better steward of our resources.

I will never forget the first time I visited the Holocaust Memorial Museum in Washington, DC, and had the sobering experience of learning more about this horrific chapter of world history. Not only did it give me a new perspective and bring to life what I had read in books, but it also changed the way I saw other people. I remember walking out the door of the museum; entering a bustling, hurried crowd of people, each one coming from somewhere different and going somewhere different; and looking at them all as if I were seeing humanity for the first time.

Instances like these change the entirety of our perspective. With our new life in Christ being the greatest of these life-changing encounters, it should be no surprise to us that Jesus came to change not just who we are but also how we see things. Because of Jesus, you and I now have a new lens through which to view ourselves, others, and the world.

How We See Ourselves

It's not enough to simply say hello to the new life God gives us; we must embrace our new vision, which changes the way we see ourselves.

In previous chapters we've practiced breaking up with ourselves, leaving behind old identities, and turning away from futile sources of security. But we are called to go even a step further. We must view ourselves as no longer our own. While the world and our sin nature train us to say, "I am my own person; I answer to no one," God says, "You are my precious adopted child. You now belong to me."

What does it mean to fully belong to God? The Bible speaks so extensively on the subject, it's actually hard to know where to begin! But let's dig in and uncover some truths about our place in the world with this miraculous, new God-given vision.

1. We See Ourselves as More

The apostle John enthusiastically declared in his first epistle, "What great love the Father has lavished on us, that we should be called children of God!" (1 John 3:1 NIV). We have found a permanent place of belonging in the family of God, not because of our own efforts but due to the *lavish* love of God the Father.

Paul tells us something similarly wonderful. He wrote that we are no longer slaves but sons and daughters of God, and his very heirs (Gal. 4:6–7). At the time he wrote this in his letter to the Christians in Galatia, many religious leaders were advocating for the acceptance of Christ as Lord *and* the continued belief that keeping the Law—the rules they dutifully sought to follow—offset the penalty of death they knew was due them because of sinful human nature. When Paul declared that these believers were no longer slaves, he was saying that Jesus had taken on the death penalty himself and had paid the price for them. And whoever belonged to him would no longer be subject to the weight of keeping all their man-made rules. Jesus had come to set them free!

Let's listen to one last word from Paul that further reveals our family status in God's eyes:

> Don't forget that you Gentiles used to be outsiders. . . . You were excluded from citizenship among the people of Israel, and you did not know the covenant promises God had made to them. You lived in this world without God and without hope. But now you have been united with Christ Jesus. Once you were far away from God, but now you have been brought near to him through the blood of Christ. (Eph. 2:11–13 NLT)

It is almost too much to bear to consider what my life would look like "far away" from Christ—without hope or a future, without the comfort of his presence, the daily guidance of his Spirit, or the promise of this new life I have come to know.

But now, because of the Father's great love for us and the sacrifice of Jesus on the cross, I see myself as forever his, forever treasured. I have a place of belonging in his family.

2. We See Ourselves as Less

But there is a responsibility that comes with such belonging. *Responsibility?* you may be thinking. *I thought you just said that Christ's sacrifice on the cross is a free gift.* Yes. And no.

I'll explain what I mean with a story. The church where I work also houses a school that three of my four kids now attend. The building consists of three main levels and a terrace, which houses all the worship and music offices. They call it a terrace to make us feel better, but it's really just a basement. And I'm okay with that.

My office is located about twenty feet from the school music room, which is delightful on days the children are sweetly singing "Jesus Loves Me" or playing Brahms to learn about orchestral music. But there is a certain time in the school year when the students get to learn how to play their first instrument: the recorder. My kids haven't reached that level of musical prowess yet, and I'm sure it's endearing to hear your child play you a song on this flute-like instrument, but our experience on the other side of the wall is a bit different. From 8:00 a.m. to 3:00 p.m. we hear not in-tune, pleasant recorder playing, but seven God-forsaken hours of an intolerable, out-of-tune version of "Hot Cross Buns" played over and over and over until I can even hear it at home in my sleep.

After several weeks of music lessons, I finally reached my limit and found myself barging into the school music room, grabbing the pink plastic recorder from little Susie's sweet fingers, and breaking it in half over my knee! Actually I didn't do that, but I did pass one of the classrooms and gave the students a nice eye roll. Yes, Laura Story, a worship leader at Perimeter Church, rolled her eyes at a group of ten-year-olds for playing their recorders. I am a despicable person.

I share this story with you not to ask for prayer for those of us who have offices on the terrace level of the church. (We've since invested in earplugs and joined a recovery group.) I confess this to you because I was clearly out of line.

Before I enter our building each day, I am required to put on a name badge for security purposes. It simply says my name and

Perimeter Church. The day I wanted to throw mine in the work-room shredder, I could sense the Lord telling me, *When you put on this name tag, you are not just naming yourself; you are also representing me. Because of that, your actions toward others should reflect how I feel about them. Laura, you belong to me now.*

Though I've been thankful many days since for the visual reminder of a church name badge, the truth is that whether or not I am wearing it, in our church building or while I'm checking out at my local supermarket, I no longer represent just myself. I belong to someone and something greater.

I no longer represent just myself. I belong to someone and something greater.

Another way to think of this belonging is through the privileges and responsibilities of being part of a family. Although some days I wonder how wise it was of God to put these adorable human beings in our charge, Martin's and my children are under our care. Much like in our relationship with the Lord, they enjoy the many perks of belonging. They are provided for, which means our eight-, six-, six-, and two-year-olds aren't expected to get jobs—not yet anyway. They enjoy free lodging, warm beds, three meals a day, and free unsolicited advice on any number of topics! We do our best to teach them about faith, relationships, money, life, and whatever else we can during the short eighteen years we have them under our roof. But that provision and care does not come without expectations.

Our children know our home is not a democracy but a monarchy. Martin and I have established rules and standards by which we live, and most of these are not optional. Our toddlers do not decide their own curfew. And all the kids do chores; even little Timmy has learned to unload a few items from the dishwasher without shattering them. Yes, we show abounding grace when our kids miss the mark, but sometimes our love for them is shown *by* disciplining them. It's simply part of what it means to belong to our family.

Probably the best scripture for understanding the implications of this belonging is found in Galatians: "Those who belong to Christ Jesus have crucified the flesh with its passions and desires. If we live by the Spirit, let us also keep in step with the Spirit" (5:24–25). I am not a Greek scholar, although I love to flip through a lexicon when I'm having trouble understanding a passage. If I'm reading a verse that is either confusing or discomforting, the tension eases once I delve deeper into the author's original language. But when I dig deeper into the word Paul used to describe our appropriate posture toward our passions and desires that are of the flesh, what I find in the Greek is just as brutal as the word used in the English translation. It's as if Jesus addressed his children through Paul's writing, saying, "If you belong to me, your flesh must be *crucified*"—which is the word used to describe Jesus' body impaled on a cross.

Paul didn't say we should set our fleshly desires aside. He didn't ask us to rein in or lessen those desires. He put it simply: our old ways must die.

Please don't misunderstand. This isn't a judgment on your value, your personality traits, or your Enneagram number. God delights in how uniquely he created each of us. He not only loves you—he *likes* you, more than you could dare to dream! Remember the high price Jesus paid to redeem you? That's actually why it's appropriate for us to respond by putting to death our lesser desires, the ones that are self-focused, self-damaging, and a damning result of the fall we read about in Genesis 3.

But good news! In the same verse in Galatians 5, we learn it's the death to our desires that brings to life a new desire—to be in step with the Spirit! And crucifying our fleshly desires gives way to the Spirit doing his redeeming work in our hearts. We kill our desire to be first, to be renowned, to be right, to be in charge, to be respected, and to be in control. Every ability we have and every possession we own has been claimed and enlisted for a greater cause than ourselves. We are fully his.

Isn't that freeing? Rather than carrying around the banner of "Laura," I can fully take on the posture of Jesus. Rather than pursuing a vision of escaping the pain of the cross, Jesus, as always, deferred to the vision of his Father: "Hallowed be *your* name. *Your* kingdom come, *your* will be done, on earth as it is in heaven" (Matt. 6:9–10, emphasis added).

Another passage that helps us understand this great and mysterious new vision for our lives is Romans 6. The entire chapter gives a fuller picture, but let's consider these four verses:

> What then? Are we to sin because we are not under law but under grace? By no means! Do you not know that if you present yourselves to anyone as obedient slaves, you are slaves of the one whom you obey, either of sin, which leads to death, or of obedience, which leads to righteousness? But thanks be to God, that you who were once slaves of sin have become obedient from the heart to the standard of teaching to which you were committed, and, having been set free from sin, have become slaves of righteousness. (vv. 6:15–18)

Paul did not mince words. In fact, he spoke quite plainly: each of us is either a slave to sin or a servant of God. Thanks be to God, we have been freed from sin's power over us, freed to live lives of godliness and righteousness. Freed to replace our old, fleshly desires with new desires that align with God's heart. But in this freedom, we do not remain masterless. We voluntarily submit our lives to the authority of Jesus, every piece of who we are. Jon Bloom describes this reality well, reflecting on Paul's words on the subject in 1 Corinthians 6:19–20.

> A bond-slave is not his own person. He has sold himself to some-one else. He belongs to someone else. He does not merely do as he pleases. His time is not his own. He is not free to follow the whims of his personal dreams. He is not free to indulge the crav-ing of his appetites as he wishes. He is not his own. He belongs to his Master. This is what a Christian is.[1]

As we say hello to a new vision, this vision changes the way we see ourselves. We are no longer our own. We belong to Christ. Just in case you are tempted to think this idea of God's authority over our lives is heavy-handed or oppressive, consider the following fictitious story.

A neighborhood boy gets in a fight with his parents and walks to the park down the street to blow off some steam. He sits down next to a boy about his age who, unbeknownst to him, is an orphan. The neighborhood boy begins to complain about how harshly he is being treated in his home. First, he complains about curfew.

"They expect me to be home by 11:00 p.m.!" he exclaims. "Who has ever heard of such lame restrictions?!"

"I don't have a curfew at all. No one expects me to be home at any time," the orphan replies.

"And I'm grounded for my grades!" the boy continues. "My par-ents are so concerned with me getting a college scholarship, they aren't letting me out of their sight till I can maintain a B average."

"No one has ever grounded me. I can get whatever grades I want," the orphan replies.

"And the constant chores! Clean your room, help your little

sister with her homework, it's your turn to clean up the table from dinner. I feel like I'm their servant or something!"

"I have no chores, no family responsibilities, no table to clean from dinner," the orphan replies.

Man, that kid sure is lucky, thinks the neighbor boy as he heads back to his home and his family.

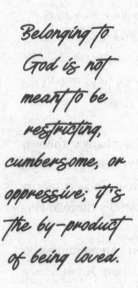

Belonging to God is not meant to be restricting, cumbersome, or oppressive; it's the by-product of being loved.

Sure, this story is fictitious, but it highlights a certain truth. Belonging to God is not meant to be restricting, cumbersome, or oppressive; it's the by-product of being loved. Belonging is the by-product of being wanted.

God saw you, my friend. His heart was moved with compassion, and he chose you—for his family, for his purposes, and ultimately to reside and reign with him in his glory. Belonging to an almighty God is the greatest privilege known to man, and we get to enjoy this privilege for eternity!

3. We See Others Differently

Just as receiving new vision dramatically changes the way we see ourselves, it also reshapes the way we view and interact with others.

Martin is one of the most endearing people I have ever met. One of his greatest attributes is how he seeks to honor veterans and others who serve in law enforcement roles. We have a fire station near our home, and the kids will often make cookies for the firefighters on duty. I once overheard Martin thanking a mall cop for his service. I chastised him a bit for it. "Really? Were you thanking him for making sure no one was stealing those Gap models or riding the escalators backward?!" But as usual, my shallow comments only exposed how ungrateful a person I am. The truth is, Martin seeks to make every person feel special, regardless of their role or title.

There's much we could all learn from that. What if, when we looked at the people around us, we saw the *imago Dei*, the image of God in each of them? What if we could see them the way God sees them?

The apostle Paul wrote one of the most arresting (no pun intended) passages I have found in the Scriptures concerning how we view others: "Do nothing from selfish ambition or conceit, but in humility count others more significant than yourselves. Let each of you look not only to his own interests, but also to the interests of others" (Phil. 2:3–4).

I can't imagine a more abnormal attitude to adopt. Think of others above myself? Are you serious? Even if we concede to this being a reasonable expectation, we have to admit that this is not something that comes naturally. We have already touched on our innate desire to put ourselves first, but what is it about others that should compel us to elevate their interests above our own?

When we read about the creation of humanity in Genesis, you'll recall that it didn't just say we were crafted by God's hands. It said we were created by God *in his image*. This obviously doesn't mean we were born with all his attributes and power, but it does speak to our value as humans. There is a special dignity embedded in us, reserved for humanity alone. Granted, when we look around at all that is going on in our culture, we may question whether that image still exists. It does! Even after the fall, we still bear God's image. It may be disfigured or distorted (much like normal has been distorted), but the *imago Dei* in us is no less true even in its distortion.

What does this have to do with how we treat others? With our new vision of self and others, we must also see others as image bearers of God. They have dignity that is worthy of being called out in their lives. I do not mean to get political here, but this is the core belief behind every effort to protecting lives, liberating lives, and preserving lives. Every single life at every age; of every ethnicity, nationality, language, and faith; in every socioeconomic class carries the *imago Dei*. The great turning point for our hearts is when we learn to see it in them as Jesus does.

Why is it so hard to live in light of this magnificent truth? What makes it such a challenge to see God reflected in those around us? I believe there are literally millions of people who have settled for lives that are so much less than what God designed for them. It is sad but true that many who are in darkness aren't even aware they have the potential within them for a life of significance. Many don't yet know that their days on earth were ordained.

Too many have never known the kind affections of someone looking out for their interests. They've never had a champion, an advocate they work with through life's challenges. They live without hope. When they consider their future, they do not dream of good things to come.

"Hope deferred makes the heart sick" (Prov. 13:12). Let this proverb saturate you with empathy; then let's consider how we can use the resources God has entrusted to us for the benefit of others.

If you've experienced new life, you have a wonderful opportunity to share this with others. Maybe through kind, nonjudgmental words, or by sharing a meal with someone, or by purchasing someone a new pair of shoes. However you are living out this new life, Paul called this being ambassadors. He tells us, "We are ambassadors for Christ, God making his appeal through us. We implore you on behalf of Christ, be reconciled to God" (2 Cor. 5:20).

How God Sees the World

In the next chapter we'll talk more about the new mission God has called us to. But it begins with a clear understanding of how God sees the world and how different that vision is from the normal way we've grown up seeing it.

Clearly God must be a fan of the world; he fashioned it himself! But we know that his initial design for creation was marred by sin. The fall fractured and corrupted our earth, so we only see glimpses of what God intended. Still, his love and commitment to our world hasn't changed. The very first Bible verse most of us ever learned as kids still rings true today: "For God *so loved* the world, that he gave his only Son, that whoever believes in him should not perish but have eternal life" (John 3:16, emphasis added). His love for our world is still that great and unfathomable.

God's heart for the world is seen in both the Old and New Testaments. It has never changed! In Genesis 12, God called Abraham and promised to make from him a great nation, describing the multitude of this nation being like stars in the sky. What was the purpose of this nation? For Abraham's fame? For sheer numbers and force? No. "I will make of you a great nation, and I will bless you and make your name great, *so that you will be a blessing*" (Gen. 12:2, emphasis added).

I heard this teaching for the first time when I was in college, and it radically changed forever how I would see the world. It rocked my understanding of what it meant to be a Christian. God has chosen us and blessed us, not to just sit around as his favored ones, doing Bible studies and attending Christian events. He blessed so we could be a blessing to the world around us! I had always known this to be the teaching of Jesus, but I was stunned to find it in Genesis. This really was God's plan from the beginning!

But what does this mean for us? We are often told to be in the world but not of it, so what does this look like practically? Let's look at Jesus' words:

> Jesus went throughout all the cities and villages, teaching in their synagogues and proclaiming the gospel of the kingdom and healing every disease and every affliction. When he saw the crowds, he had compassion for them, because they were harassed and helpless, like sheep without a shepherd. Then he said to his disciples, "The harvest is plentiful, but the laborers are few; therefore pray earnestly to the Lord of the harvest to send out laborers into his harvest." (Matt. 9:35–38)

A few things to notice. Jesus was traveling through villages and cities, and "when he saw the crowds" he felt compassion. In these verses we are able to view the world directly through God's eyes! Why compassion? Because he saw their true state—"harassed and helpless, like sheep without a shepherd." Commentator John Phillips described Jesus as being "stirred by their plight." He wrote, "[Jesus'] response was not merely an intellectual assessment of the situation of the earth's millions. His response was that of a tender shepherd."[2]

Can I ask you something that might seem a bit personal? When was the last time you felt compassion toward the world? When I speak of the world, I speak collectively, including the vast majority of people who do not know Jesus.

Ask yourself, *Do I think of them with the tender thoughts of a shepherd? When someone gives me an unkind hand gesture in traffic, or a neighbor acts cold toward me, or a school bully says degrading things to my child, how do I respond? Am I readying myself to attack and defend, filled with anger? Or do I see others through the eyes of*

Jesus, loving those who do not know the tender Shepherd I know?
Lord, give us your vision for the world.

New Sight Takes Us New Places

The verses in Matthew 9 don't just call us to *see* the world differently; they call us to go. God is asking us to engage, to move forward in compassion, to take part in his redemptive work.

Having been a Christian most of my life, I'm still amazed at how diverse our views as believers tend to be toward the world. I've noticed that some groups completely withdraw from culture. For the sake of piety, they disengage from the world around them. Their slogan might as well be "Let's hunker down in this church building until Jesus comes back."

Other Christians embrace the world too much, to the point that their lives as believers are indistinguishable from the lives of unbelievers. Their slogan might be "Live it up. God gave us this world to enjoy!"

The truth is that neither of these views represents how God sees the world, or how he calls us to see the world. In one of Jesus' most in-depth sermons about the Christian life, he told his followers to be salt and light in the world. He didn't mean we should throw salt *at* people, spouting Bible verses or tossing well-meaning tracts out of our car windows while we stay safe in our Christian cocoons, awaiting the glorious rapture. Nor should we shine glaringly bright lights in people's eyes that blind them and send them staggering.

He said to *be* salt and light, engaging in our world for its flourishing. And he warned us not to lose our saltiness. "You are the salt of the earth, but if salt has lost its taste, how shall its saltiness be restored?" (Matt. 5:13). There is so much more that could be said about this passage, but my main point is to highlight the relationship Jesus called us to have with the world. Is it a strange balance? Yes! Is it abnormal compared to the rest of the world? Yes! Is it God's model for how his people might join him in his work of redemption? For sure!

Let's reflect one last time on Jesus' words in Matthew 9. He described a field. Keep in mind that he was speaking to a more agrarian culture than you may live in, so he was probably describing a field that was sitting right in front of his listeners. We may have to use our imaginations. Imagine a field of corn, or just pick your favorite vegetable here. I am clearly not a farmer, but I assume that an important part of farming is having enough farmhands to collect the full yield of crops in a timely fashion.

This is the picture Jesus painted, only the yield of the crop was more plentiful than the numbers of workers available to reap it. So what did he ask? He asked the disciples to pray for laborers—to go out and collect the harvest.

What I'm describing here is what we will call *mission* in the next chapter. It is God's exciting invitation to join him where he is already at work. But before we can consider how we might use our hands and feet, we must embrace God's vision, using our eyes. Because a person ready for the mission is one who sees things others might not see.

Are you ready for this mission, seeing your life as no longer your own, seeing others as created in God's image, and seeing the world as ripe for harvest? Read this prayer with me, written by Puritans centuries ago, and let's use it to help ready our hearts.

SOVEREIGN GOD,
Thy cause, not my own, engages my heart,
    and I appeal to thee with greatest freedom
to set up thy kingdom in every place

where Satan reigns;
Glorify thyself and I shall rejoice,
    for to bring honour to thy name is my sole desire.
I adore thee that thou art God,
        and long that others should know it, feel it,
            and rejoice in it.
O that all men might love and praise thee,
        that thou mightiest have all glory
            from the intelligent world!
Let sinners be brought to thee for thy dear name!
To the eye of reason everything respecting
        the conversion of others is as dark as midnight,
But thou canst accomplish great things;
        the cause is thine,
        and it is to thy glory that men should be saved.
Lord, use me as thou wilt,
        do with me what thou wilt;
            but, O, promote thy cause,
let thy kingdom come,
let thy blessed interest be advanced
        in this world!
O do thou bring in great numbers to Jesus!
        let me see that glorious day,
        and give me to grasp for multitudes of souls;
        let me be willing to die to that end;
and while I live let me labour for thee
        to the utmost of my strength,
        spending time profitably in this work,
        both in health and in weakness.
It is thy cause and kingdom I long for,
        not my own.[3]

I pray that these words will birth a new vision within us. May we no longer view our lives as our own but as an offering to bring before the Lord each day. May we view others no longer for what they might do for us but for how we might serve and bless them. And as we see the world around us, may we neither dive in, consuming its pleasures, nor turn from it in disgust or indifference. May we see the world as God sees it and be moved toward it with compassion. Amen.

Chapter Ten

Hello, New Mission

While I was attending Columbia International University, I met two guys, Shane and Warren, who had just started a band. They mentioned to me one weekend that their bass player had to miss a *gig*. This was a new word for me, having grown up playing string bass in orchestra. We just called a performance, well, a *performance*.

Anyway, Shane and Warren asked if I wanted to do this gig with them, and although I didn't really know what I was signing up for, it sounded, by far, like the coolest thing I'd ever been asked to be part of. I said yes, and for five years I was part of a band called Silers Bald.

Meanwhile, I continued to write songs and eventually went back to touring, which led to this lifelong God-given career assignment as a singer, songwriter, and speaker, which I have absolutely loved. My greatest joy comes from sharing songs and stories that somehow bring hope to people processing how real life and real faith intersect. In this work, I've been privileged to write and tour with bands and artists I grew up listening to on the radio. Amazing! Yet for every story of an award won or a shiny stage with a cheering audience, I can tell you ten more stories a whole lot less glamorous.

Fast-forward to a few years ago when Martin and I discovered we were having twins. I've always known God's mission for me was to be a family affair—which means that as our family grows, so must our vehicle. Luckily my manager found us a great deal on a converted black Sprinter van that came complete with TV, microwave, fridge, and five bunks in the back. After baby-proofing the bunks and filling all the cubbies with diapers and bottles, we were set!

This past spring, while we were heading back from an event, a tire blew out on the Sprinter in the backwoods of Kentucky. We were truly in the middle of nowhere, and it was nearly midnight. The only place open at that hour was an old, dilapidated truck stop that was being remodeled.

I woke up our four sleeping kids, and we unloaded while our trusty bandmates worked on the bum tire. After ten minutes of playing freeze tag with the kids in the parking lot, I decided it would be safer to take them inside the truck stop. There I found a sweet night-shift cashier who allowed them to play on the video poker machines, even though none of them were eighteen.

I have to laugh when people say to me, "Life on the road must be so glamorous!" because I always carry a mental picture of my children in their pajamas, eating Cheetos, and pretending to play video poker well past midnight.

The truth is, I wouldn't trade those moments for anything in the world—every flat tire, production malfunction, weather-related airport layover, piece of luggage lost (resulting in my children running around venues in their diapers). Every bit of joy and misfortune has been part of the mission to which God has called our family. It has not been normal, but it has been an adventure. It has built character in my children. It has built character in me.

When we say goodbye to normal, we don't just receive a new life. We receive a new mission.

Usually when we hear the word *mission*, our minds go to one of two places. For those who grew up Baptist, it's to collecting loose change in fake paper rice bowls for the Lottie Moon Christmas Offering. For others, it's the Tom Cruise action movies: "Your mission, should you choose to accept it, is to accept your fate. . . . Good luck, Mr. Hunt. This message will self-destruct in five seconds."[1]

When I speak of mission, I'm speaking of a calling God places on your life. This could be as drastic as a commission overseas to serve in another country or as simple as meeting neighbors in your apartment complex. It's not so much where you go but the intentionality by which you live in the place you already find yourself. It's living each moment with gospel purpose.

How has God gifted you? How might you use those gifts for gospel purposes? That's mission! It could be writing and sharing songs as I do, or being willing to share with others your journey with cancer. It could be opening your home to foster children or to college kids who just need a home-cooked meal and a washer and dryer. I have a good friend who is an incredible harp player. Her mission was taking early retirement and starting a harp-equine therapy ministry that helps children who have gone through trauma. That's the exciting part about living on mission. It will look different for each person, based on your unique gifting, background, resources, and stage of life. But it starts with your willingness to live out this new vision. It starts with saying hello to a new mission.

Our family set a goal of completing twenty hikes in 2020. And like most milestones in twenty-first-century life, we forever memorialized it with the Instagram hashtag #20hikesin2020. I can proudly say that we hiked in rain, ice, and snow until we finally met our goal, having hiked more than forty-five miles together in a span of nine months! But before you applaud our efforts, I need to admit that our plan backfired.

Martin and I truly hoped to cultivate within our kids a deeper love for the outdoors and a hunger for adventure. Our final hike of the year was to Laurel Falls in the Great Smoky Mountains. When we reached the coveted destination, I pulled out my camera to capture the perfect nostalgic moment to honor and celebrate our momentous accomplishment. That was also the exact moment my kids began to chant in unison, "No more hikes! No. More. Hikes!" While we had intended to inspire them to become lifelong hikers, instead we had turned them into worn-out, burnt-out ramblers who wanted nothing more than to watch movies for the remaining Saturdays of 2020.

Here is what I want you to see about mission. Our family set a goal, requiring us to reallocate some of our time and reshape our schedule a bit. We didn't start out like the movie version of the von Trapp family, hiking over the Swiss Alps. We took baby steps, and we sought to take them consistently in the same direction. Forty-five miles later, we had gone from a family who spent most of our weekends watching Netflix to a family who spent a large amount of time outdoors.

He Shoulders the Load

Not only is God's mission a journey rather than a sprint, but it is also not a solo endeavor embarked upon in our own strength. This again brings to mind Hebrews 12. We looked at this chapter earlier, but it's helpful to revisit it as we say hello to a new mission.

> Therefore, since we also have such a great a cloud of witnesses surrounding us, let's rid ourselves of every obstacle and the sin which so easily entangles us, and let's run with endurance the

race that is set before us, looking only at Jesus, the originator and perfecter of the faith, who for the joy set before Him endured the cross, despising the shame, and has sat down at the right hand of the throne of God.

For consider Him who has endured such hostility by sinners against Himself, so that you will not grow weary and lose heart. (vv. 1–3 NASB)

I have often been reminded that when we come across the word *therefore* in the Bible, it's appropriate to ask, "What is it there for?" In this case, "therefore" is a call to remember all the men and women who have come before the persecuted Jewish believers to whom this letter was addressed. We're to remember their victories, setbacks, and sufferings, and to recall the ways God was faithful through it all. To see these historical men and women as examples of godly faith. This was written to inspire and encourage our faith for the long haul, as well as to motivate us to intentionally, and with wisdom and understanding, lay down anything hindering our progress as we set out—on a race, or a family hike, or our divine mission.

Maybe your heart becomes anxious as you think about your personal mission in this race that is set before us. That's entirely understandable, particularly if you think it depends on you and your effort alone. But what does this passage say is the key to anything we're asked to endure? First, we're to fix our eyes on Jesus. He is the one writing this story of redemption—the one strengthening us for all that comes our way. Second, whatever we face as we step into this mission, Jesus has already experienced, endured, and

Whatever we face as we step into this mission, Jesus has already experienced, endured, and completed.

completed. He knows what's ahead, and he will make sure we have the faith and strength to complete the mission.

Let's pause a moment here. Perhaps today you're feeling so maxed out that to even think about a "new mission" has you breaking out in hives. Maybe you feel the way my kids felt. *No. More. Hikes!* Maybe you feel as Jean Fleming described:

> "Surely the Christian life was meant to be simpler than this," a friend complained to her husband. I agree. In the twenty some years I've been a Christian, I've received instruction on and been challenged to read my Bible daily, pray without ceasing, do in-depth Bible study regularly, memorize Scripture, meditate day and night, fellowship with other believers, always be ready to give an answer to the questioning unbeliever, give to missions, and to the poor, work as unto the Lord, use my time judiciously, give thanks in all circumstances, serve the Body using my gifts to edify others, keep a clean house as a testimony, practice gracious hospitality, submit to my husband, love and train my children, disciple other women, manage my finances as a good steward, involve myself in school and community activities, develop and maintain non-Christian friendships, stimulate my mind with careful reading, improve my health through diet and exercise, color coordinate my wardrobe, watch my posture, and "simplify" my life by baking my own bread.[2]

You may read this and laugh. Or perhaps for you it's a pretty accurate description of what it feels like to be a Christian. *How can I possibly live up to such expectations? Yes, I want to be on mission. But I'm not Superwoman! I'm just one person already feeling stretched thin.*

Hear me, friend: the beauty of anything God calls us to is that it was never intended to be burdensome. Jesus spoke directly to this faulty thinking.

> Come to me, all who labor and are heavy laden, and I will give you rest. Take my yoke upon you, and learn from me, for I am gentle and lowly in heart, and you will find rest for your souls. For my yoke is easy, and my burden is light. (Matt. 11:28–30)

He didn't say, "Come to me so I can put you to work." He didn't say, "Come to me so I can weigh you down with unrealistic expectations." He called out to those who were wearied from life not to saddle them with more responsibilities and add to their weariness but to tell them to rest. Jesus is not a tyrannical taskmaster. He is quite the opposite. He described himself as *gentle*. Lowly in heart. And his yoke? Picture a single harness used for two oxen. This is the picture Jesus painted for us.

We are always together with him, working toward the same goal, a common mission. And now imagine that our co-laborer is in fact the Lord of the universe, who made the heavens and the earth. If we are on mission, partnering with an omnipotent God, how hard could our labor be? Yes, we will toil on our mission and sometimes be stretched to our limits physically or emotionally. But God does the heavy lifting. We'll labor in his power, not our own. This is how the believer finds rest, even while serving. God is, after all, our shepherd, who restores our souls (Ps. 23).

He Conquers Our Reluctance

I understand if you still resist the idea of being "on mission." Even though mission doesn't always involve a change in geography, it always involves a change. Living on mission always means adjusting our lives, including how we spend our time, our money, and our talents. When we are honest with ourselves, isn't it easier to just keep things normal?

All this is to say, if you are feeling reluctant, you are in good company. The good news is that the Bible doesn't just give us instruction; it gives us stories! Let me share five inspiring illustrations with you. Trust me—there are many more, but we'll focus especially on those who were hesitant to step into the redemption story and assume the roles God handcrafted for them.

First, let's go back to Exodus. If there was ever a more reluctant deliverer than Moses,[3] I would be surprised. He gave every excuse in the book for avoiding the mission God had assigned to him, all of which God dismissed. In the end Moses went back to Egypt to deliver the Israelites, but not without bringing his brother, Aaron, along with him.

A little later in the biblical narrative, we read of Gideon in the book of Judges.[4] His great stalling tactic was to insist God give him a sign, or a "fleece." If the fleece he laid out became wet overnight, he would take it as confirmation that God was indeed calling him to go. Guess what? He woke up, checked the fleece, and was able to squeeze a full bowl of water from it. So off he went to accept his assignment from the Lord, right? Nope. He did it again, this time asking God to keep the fleece *dry* overnight. Next day, the ground was wet, but the fleece was dry. Finally, he accepted his mission.

Frankly, I'm a lot like Gideon. I am always asking for a sign, something that will make my walk of faith just a little more of a walk of sight.

Let's move on to the book of Isaiah.[5] When Isaiah encountered God, he was immediately struck by his own unworthiness. He knew all too well that he was ill suited to represent God. I have felt this way more times than I care to count. I know that I, too, am one of "unclean lips" (6:5). But over the years I have learned to take God at his word and believe by faith that my guilt has been taken away and my sin has been forgiven (v. 7).

If I can do it, anyone can learn to say along with Isaiah, "Here I am! Send me," when God asks, "Whom shall I send?" (v. 8).

Flipping to the next book after Isaiah, we read of the prophet Jeremiah.[6] Jeremiah's case wasn't so much one of reluctance. And as I read his story, I observe how God gently and carefully worked through different scenarios with Jeremiah, despite what seem to be fairly valid concerns and anxieties. Isn't it interesting that when God commissioned Jeremiah, he looked back through time and said, "Before you were born I consecrated you; I appointed you a prophet to the nations" (Jer. 1:5)?

I don't know about you, but this gives me great comfort. God's plan A and my role in that plan has been known long before I ever stepped into the story. As God spoke to Jeremiah, he addressed the same issues common to us: Youthfulness. Fear. Inexperience as a public speaker. And on and on. God dealt with every objection Jeremiah raised. But as with the others called by God, in the end Jeremiah did as he was instructed.

I can attest that God has dealt with every excuse I've raised whenever I have tried to sidestep a mission.

This last example comes from a New Testament passage many of us are familiar with and could probably recite from memory. Let's look at the Great Commission.[7] Jesus had finished his earthly ministry, and he was in his postresurrection body. Now it was time to turn the ministry over to his disciples. The disciples headed to Galilee, to the mountain where Jesus instructed them to wait for him. Jesus met them there, and they enjoyed a time of worship before Jesus gave them (and us) those famous words of commission: "All authority in heaven and on earth has been given to Me. Go, therefore, and make disciples of all the nations" (Matt. 28:18–19 NASB).

Recall that the disciples had been with Jesus for about three years. They'd observed his humanity as well as his divinity. They'd seen him crucified. They'd seen him buried. And now they were witnesses to his resurrection. You'd think they must have been walking on the clouds, brimming with confidence. But this text gives us some insight into the state of their hearts. In verse 17, we read that "some were doubtful" (NASB).

Honestly, I get it. I suspect if I were with them on that mountainside, I'd be a complete wreck, thumbing through my Moleskine, checking my notes to see if anything was missing. *Okay, what do I do when I come across people possessed by demons? I need pigs, and a lake. Blindness? Dirt and some spittle. Oh my, I know I have forgotten something. Hang on, did Jesus just say, "Go to the nations?" I don't remember him saying that when he recruited us!* I can totally empathize with the disciples who doubted.

If you're feeling as if God is calling you to something that is too big, something for which you're not fully equipped, remember, the disciples who doubted *went*, in the power of the Holy Spirit. And it was said of them, "These men who have turned the world upside down have come here also" (Acts 17:6). How do you feel about getting in on some action that might turn the world upside down?

Okay, that may be a little ambitious. But really, when we step into our divine roles within the story of redemption, God *will* do something remarkable in and through us. As unsure as you may be, he will never draw you into anything for which he won't also provide every resource. So go ahead, take your excuses to Jesus. I bet he has already heard them. Let him comfort you and give you the confidence to press on.

He Offers Eternity

There is much to be done in our world today. There are endless dark places where the light of the gospel is needed. Go, even in the face of resistance. Many will show little or no interest in the things of God. The world has shown them a distorted understanding of eternal things. They're being sold the promise that the very best that life has to offer is available to us here and now. Shine your light anyway. Show them the love of Christ. And always remember: our job is not to change hearts and minds. Only God can do that. Our job is to go.

Our call, the call of missions, is to live out, in word and deed, the reality of eternity. When we truly believe what the Bible taught regarding life, death, heaven, and hell, sharing Jesus with a dying world is no longer optional.

> *Our job is not to change hearts and minds. Only God can do that. Our job is to go.*

To that end, I would like to give you a glimpse of eternity with God. I think after you read this description, you will want to step into your role in his unfolding story of redemption. As I read these words, I cannot help but get excited about what awaits us. Please do not mistake this for "pie in the sky by and by" or Pollyannaish thinking. When I speak about being tethered in the middle of our trials, and when I recommend this tremendous Christian life, I mean more than the life you are presently living. I'm also thinking of the life that is to come.

As you read these words, sit back and visualize. Allow them to wash over your soul. Speak them aloud and let them linger on your tongue like fresh honey from a hive.

What will heaven be like?

Heaven is where we dream and grow and play and work along with all the redeemed saints. Whatever our occupation in heaven, there will be maximum satisfaction, enjoyment and pleasure, of the kind we have only glimpsed here and now. Laughter, accomplishment, fulfillment—being who we were made to be, achieving our full potential, and discovering a contentment that is wonderful (that is, full of wonder), is what heaven is about.

In its final form, heaven is a new earth. Mountains, oceans, rivers, lakes, forests, sandy beaches, birds, fish, animals of every kind.

And dogs. Sweet dogs to play and run with! All God's creation now restored. For us to explore and investigate and try to understand. That means science, and travel, and composition, and art, and music, and poetry; all that is pure and lovely and good. New talents to learn (I do hope so). New experiences to enjoy.

And all of it, forever and ever.

And the face of Jesus!

The greatest experience of heaven will be to gaze on Jesus's beautiful face. "They will see his face" (Rev. 22:4).

To look at Him with tears of joy and say, "Thank you, sweet Jesus. Thank you!"

And bow in worship and praise and adoration and sing His praises.[8]

I recently came across this quote: "For those not in Christ, this life is the best it will ever get. For those in Christ, for whom Ephesians 2:7 is the eternal vista just around the next bend in the road, this life is the worst it will ever get."[9] This may sound harsh, but I believe it's true. Not that I am so focused on heaven that I've already checked out of this life. Far from it. In fact, as I read this description of heaven, I want to embrace any mission the Lord puts in front of me with greater intensity and commitment.

Do you, like me, want to share this wonderful gift with as many people as you can? If they only knew what awaited them!

It Starts Today

I invite you to say hello to a new mission, with eternity as both the goal and the ultimate prize. Maybe as you are reading these words, your mind is firing like crazy, considering all the things to which God might be calling you.

Maybe you have been here before. You have been excited, but over time you checked out after being disappointed in less-than-perfect outcomes. I want to encourage you to reconnect with Jesus' heart for others.

If you've journeyed with me through this book, honestly evaluating how to free yourself from the distractions and distortions of the world's idea of normal, you may now be in a much better position to step into your calling. Your new missional life will feature realistic expectations and an awareness that the success of your mission is not dependent on your effort alone. God is always wanting to work through us for the sake of his kingdom.

If I were standing before you right now, I would place my hands on your shoulders, look directly into your eyes, and tell you plainly, "Friend, you do not have to have it all figured out. Simply turn toward God and allow him to lead you one step at a time. I promise, you do not want to miss out on this great adventure!"

So Long, Normal Story

The Cook Family

Meet the Cooks

Andy and Martha Cook live in Peachtree Corners, Georgia, where Andy is president of Promise686, a ministry that guides churches to find and support families caring for vulnerable children, providing financial assistance, community support, and education. They have ten children.

Laura: Describe the normal you used to know.

Martha: Well, our normal started with two biological children, followed by God calling us to adopt from Ethiopia. Initially we set out to adopt one child but found out about her sibling three weeks before we traveled, so we ended up adopting two! Just when we thought we were done, with four kids, we found out we were pregnant again. We often joke that in all the adoption chaos, we forgot that we could have biological children, so our fifth snuck up on us a bit.

Andy: Even though five kids makes for a very full house, we felt we were finally at a stable place. The youngest was almost out of diapers, and we could see the light at the end of the tunnel. And that's when we got the text.

Laura: What happened in your life to bring you to the place of saying so long to normal?

Martha: With Andy running Promise686, we often hear from people who know of fostering and adopting opportunities. I've always felt very comfortable forwarding those texts or phone calls on to Andy, given he has the resources through Promise686 to connect these children to families. But that day, when I got a text about a sibling group of five needing a home, I didn't forward it on. For some crazy reason I had the thought, *Maybe these should be our kids.*

Andy: I received a text from Martha. To help you fully understand the situation, I need to tell you that I was at a Christian men's retreat for the weekend, a time that I had set aside to reconnect with God and really hear from him. It's amazing to consider God's timing in all of this! So instead of responding like I wanted to, saying, "Are you crazy?!" I gave her a more spiritual answer: "I'll pray about it."

Martha: Once Andy got home, and the more we talked and prayed about this opportunity as a couple, the more we began to feel God calling us to adopt these children. Though it didn't make much sense, God was moving our hearts in that direction, and in really strange ways! I was waking up in the middle of the night, reading verses in God's Word about the children he has for us and sensing his lead through many other crazy things. It was like we couldn't get away from it! So, with much fear and trepidation, we finally said yes.

Andy: And when we said yes, I don't want to paint the picture that both of us were completely confident in that yes, all day every day. We both had our moments of hesitation. But for me, I've walked with God long enough to know that when he calls us to something, it may be something incredibly hard, but there's always a deep sense of satisfaction in being in the center of his will. There were definitely moments when my emotions needed time to catch up with that yes, but God, in his grace, brought those feelings and desires along as well.

Laura: So you said yes. What did that first month look like?

Martha and Andy: Everything changed!

Martha: I remember in that first month after the adoption, looking outside our house and seeing about twelve cars in our driveway at all times! Our house was constantly full of contractors, friends who came over to help with laundry, and what felt like round-the-clock tutors working to get some of the kids up to speed for school. A neighbor even reported us to our neighborhood association because they thought we had opened a home business! Since moving wasn't really an option for us financially, we modified the three upstairs bedrooms into a space for the seven boys, turned our guest bedroom into a master on the main, then redid our basement for the three girls. Friends helped tear down drywall and put up partitions, with only a loose plan for what we were actually creating. It was crazy! And to top it all off, we added a big shed in the backyard to hold the excess and twelve bikes.

Laura: What has been your steady?

Martha: People. So many people stepped up to help, some just for the initial stage, some as long-termers, but always bringing what we needed when we needed it. People seemed to come out of nowhere, people we had never met before. They had just heard our story and wanted to help. Literally hundreds of people have come alongside us.

Andy: I agree. It was the people of God. And we knew they would!

We had confidence that our church would come through for us. We had seen God's people mobilize in other situations and knew that if this was of God, he would mobilize them to support us as well.

Laura: What has been your gain?

Andy: There is a depth to me that's different. The only word I can think of is *thicker*. I am thicker from walking through this. There have been seasons that have been really, really hard. There are things about God I have known to be true my whole life, but it wasn't until this adoption that I felt those things to be true, through and through, to my very core. This experience has been deepening. I have deeper faith than I had before.

Martha: I'd say for me, I've gained more peace. I no longer have to have that low-grade anxiety that I had before, because I know everything is going to work out in some weird and messy way!

Laura: You went from having five kids to ten—and you would say you have gained peace?

Martha: It is very bizarre! I think having ten kids finally brought me to the point of surrender. For so long, I had held so tightly to all the things in my life, like my kids' academics, or their emotions, or whatever I was trying to control at the time. But at some point, I started to ask myself the question, *What if I just release this to the Lord? These kids are yours anyway, God!* Honestly, I can't control outcomes, but I can influence them, so that's what I do. I parent, and I let God be God. And there's a freedom I'm finding in leaving the rest up to him.

Andy: You know, it's funny. When you take out the idea of a calling of God on your lives, none of this makes any sense. We had people tell us they thought we were making a huge mistake.

Someone actually pulled me aside and said I was messing up a good thing, referring to the happy, manageable family we had before. For some people, all they see is the cost. But God has called us to something greater, and we have seen his goodness in a way we never would have apart from this adoption journey. Yes, there is a cost, but our gain and our children's gain has been far greater. Maybe messier and more chaotic, but definitely greater.

Chapter Eleven

Hello, Unknown

No one has ever compared me to the woman in Proverbs 31, and they probably never will. I'm not a gardener or the kind of mom who sews clothes for her kids. I have much respect for anyone with those abilities, but that's not me. And I'm really okay with it.

But there is one thing about that woman that I desperately long for people to say about me. Verse 25 says, "She is clothed with strength and dignity; *she can laugh at the days to come*" (NIV, emphasis added). The New Living Translation actually says, "She laughs without fear of the future." Her strength and dignity and confidence are more than just an air about her. They are evidenced by how she views the unknown road ahead of her, the daunting adventure awaiting around the bend.

Here's what might be said of me: she is clothed in blue jeans and free T-shirts collected from church conferences, and she lies awake at night fretting about what might happen in the days to come! But I don't want this to be my description. I don't want to be anxious about the unknown. I want to laugh!

Thank you for the time you have invested in taking this journey with me. I pray that even with the silliness of some of my personal stories, through his Word you've heard from the Lord. I may be the author, but I am simply a woman seeking to let go of normal, with all its elusiveness, and embrace something way more solid and valuable. I pray I've encouraged you to step out in boldness, step away from unhealthy or overly cautious patterns of life, and truly say goodbye to anything you lean on as a substitute for true faith.

I pray that we would never again settle for normal when God's desire for us is the extraordinary. And I pray that even in times of grieving for the loss of normal, you will grieve with hope, knowing that God's plan for you is good, and he never leaves you to grieve alone.

I wish I could leave you with definitive next steps. I wish I could paint for you a clear picture of what these truths should look like played out in your own life. I wish I could give you details and framework for the new normal I am challenging you to embrace. But that's the tricky thing about the future—most of it is unknown. As we saw with the Israelites leaving Egypt, it is often easier to stay put, living a less-fulfilling normal simply because it is known. But God has called us to step out on a tremendous adventure of faith, hasn't he?

We are called to say goodbye to what's normal and hello to the unknown.

We are called to say goodbye to what's normal and hello to the unknown.

Before you get cold feet imagining Indiana Jones taking that perilous first step over a bottomless ravine in *Indiana Jones and the Last Crusade*, know that venturing into the unknown with the God who knows all is the safest place you could possibly be. Though such risk-taking often looks foolish to the world, it is an attractive quality of a follower of Christ. Such an attitude was captured by hymn writer B. B. McKinney as he saw it in returned missionary R. S. Jones. After multiple health issues, Jones was forced to return to his Alabama home from his mission field in Brazil. When asked what he would do next, Jones replied he did not know, but "wherever he leads I'll go." This truth, which birthed a world-renowned hymn, not only represents the sentiments of both Jones and McKinney. It's this core belief of Christianity that sent every missionary hero to the remotest parts of the world.[1]

If we belong to Jesus, every piece of our lives is his. We follow where he leads, even when the path is not as clear as we might wish.

On this journey into the unknown, we have three great comforts to accompany us, three gifts to steady us, no matter how perilous the landscape appears. We have a compass to guide us, community to cheer us on, and a constant Companion, who is our source of hope.

We Have a Compass

God's Word is a lamp to our feet and a daily light to our path (Ps. 119:105). But it is also so much more. Through instruction and narrative, the Bible gives us ample direction for the unknown journey ahead.

In the Old Testament we've been given story after story of God's commitment to his people, many of whom were on their own unknown journeys. We've been given God's Law, which not only teaches us how to honor him with our lives and in our relationships but also illuminates the depth of our need for a Savior, the perfect Law Keeper. We see in the Minor Prophets God's call to a people who, much like ourselves, were prone to wander. Yet God acted in faithfulness toward them, despite their unfaithfulness to him and his covenant.

The New Testament offers beautiful stories about Jesus, how he loved and how we are to love. Through his example and teaching, we learn to forgive, to sacrifice, to treat others with kindness, and to always seek first the kingdom of heaven. We learn to submit our own names, our own kingdoms, and our own glory to God's name, kingdom, and glory—a posture that's essential for our journey. We are also instructed in the Epistles how to live as new creations and as people on mission.

The disciples knew better than anyone how to embark on an unknown journey. The book of Acts records how they prayed for boldness in the midst of persecution, rejoicing all the while (Acts 4:29). Last but not least, we are given a picture of the world to come. This hope of eternity with God in a new heaven and a new earth not only brings us comfort but prompts us to reorient our hearts to his desires and commit our lives to his agenda.[2]

To embark on a faith journey with only the Bible as a compass is to start a journey with everything you could ever need. Hear the words of the psalmist, his glowing description of God's Word:

> The law of the LORD is perfect,
>   reviving the soul;
> the testimony of the LORD is sure,
>   making wise the simple;
> the precepts of the LORD are right,
>   rejoicing the heart;
> the commandment of the LORD is pure,
>   enlightening the eyes. (Ps. 19:7–8)

Consider the implications of viewing the Bible this way and how each phrase describes something needed on our faith journey.

- God's Word *revives* us when we are weary. When we don't know if we can put one foot in front of the other, God's Word is like a cool breeze or a cold spring of water, refreshing our spirits.
- God's Word is *sure* on a path that feels anything but steady. When we don't know where to go, what to do, or what to say, we're told that God's Word literally makes us wise.
- God's Word brings *joy* to our hearts. His promises infuse joy and hopefulness into the dreariest of circumstances.
- God's Word brings *light* to our eyes with its refined purity. Where the advice of others is corrupt with competing agendas and selfish tendencies, God's counsel is pure.
- God's Word is a *treasure* without comparison.

Simply put, on our journey of faith, God's Word is enough. But to understand why I compare it to a compass, we'll have to reflect on the function of a compass and consider how we use it.

A compass will not tell you where you are supposed to go. In fact, a compass won't even tell you where you are. But when you're lost, a compass will show you which direction will get you back on course.

A compass simply points to north, a fixed point around which every other location is identified. God's Word is to his people the constant north in an ever-changing culture and world. It is always true, always right, and always applicable. May God's Word forever be our compass, pointing us in the direction we should go!

We Have Community

The second gift we are given as we journey into the unknown is community. When God calls us to step out in faith, he never calls us to a solo mission. There may be moments when you are physically alone, but he has called us to always be moving toward community.

These days, the word *community* may need some definition. Biblical community represents more than a group of like-minded people. I'm not referring to having common interests, a similar upbringing, or the same political views, skin color, or beliefs concerning the effectiveness of essential oils. Biblical community is a bond that runs deeper than affinity groups or social clubs. This type of community, like everything else about Christianity, is *different*. Where possible, it should contain people of different walks of life rather than being a homogenous group. Members of a biblical community don't have to be uniform in their political, social, and economic views, but they should be able to discuss their differing views respectfully and without fear of division. Rather than fracturing a community, differing viewpoints should add rich texture, color, and beauty. When this richness of community is displayed, a watching world notices that followers of Christ are, well, *different*.

Community is not just some warm and fuzzy element of fellowship; it is a powerful apologetic to a watching world.

Paul described this kind of community, known as the church. Forgive the length of the passage. It's just too good not to share the whole thing!

I therefore, a prisoner for the Lord, urge you to walk in a manner worthy of the calling to which you have been called, with all humility and gentleness, with patience, bearing with one another in love, eager to maintain the unity of the Spirit in the bond of peace. There is one body and one Spirit—just as you were called to the one hope that belongs to your call—one Lord, one faith, one baptism, one God and Father of all, who is over all and through all and in all. (Eph. 4:1–6)

In the same way that our Father God is one, so must the church be one. The Holy Spirit has given us a bond of peace, yet we are responsible for fostering that peace by relating to one another with humility, gentleness, and patience. This is the community to which God has called us. This is the community that accompanies us as we leave normal and enter the unknown.

Jesus' disciples, postresurrection, modeled this type of community well. To describe their new normal as unknown would be quite the understatement. These men and women had left everything to follow Jesus; they had seen him crucified, buried, risen, and ascended. Now everything from their past lives was meaningless. There they were, huddled together in that upper room on the day of Pentecost, praying and waiting on God for their next step. They had left behind the religious traditions of their upbringing and had been shunned—or worse, hunted—by the religious leaders who had killed Jesus. And they were, in many ways, starting from scratch.

But they had each other. And as Jesus had promised, the Holy Spirit came upon them that day. So they stepped forward boldly in the mission God set before them.

Theirs was a true community. Luke tells us that from then on, they had "all things in common," not referring to their preferences but their possessions (Acts 2:44). They would sell belongings to take care of any needs in their community. They no longer thought of themselves as individuals but as members of a family, parts of one body.

As I reflect on my quirkiness as a middle schooler, I know that my desire to be "normal" wasn't a desire for conformity for conformity's sake. I wanted community. If I could dress like other kids, look like them, talk like them, and joke like them, I could be one of them. What's unique about the early church was that their departure from normal became their unifying characteristic. They left

What's unique about the early church was that their departure from normal became their unifying characteristic.

their normal religious community to find *true* community that ran deeper than sharing common practices or creeds. Their new community was unified by their new gospel identity and new gospel mission.

I have such fond memories of being on mission together with Josie when she was just a one-year-old. One of those experiences that was exceptionally formative for us both was a spring tour with Casting Crowns. This band has been around for a couple of decades and has seen much success, with multiple awards and more number-one songs than I can count. But what stood out for me about our time on the road with them was not how they performed onstage, but how they lived offstage. Lead singer Mark Hall, and his wife, Melanie, had made the decision long before that if God was calling them to road life, it would be as a family. At the outset, this may not sound like such a huge decision, but the implications of their conviction affected everything about how they toured.

First of all, instead of cramming twelve musicians into a bus like most bands do, they had to splurge on three buses. Also, a decision to travel with your children means a decision to homeschool them. A typical day on the road began with school in the back lounge for the older kids and playtime in the nursery for the younger ones. And when I say nursery, I'm referring to a playroom the crew set up and tore down every day, equipped with road cases full of coloring books, crayons, building blocks, and Legos.

But here's why this experience was so impactful for me. Choosing to tour as a first-time mom was choosing to leave behind every traditional thing I had ever been told to do as a mother. I was leaving behind the way I had seen my mom raise me. I couldn't take my child to regular playdates, to the library, or to our neighborhood playground. But in leaving normalcy and going on mission, I found community with other people who had left normal for the sake of mission.

Though our lifestyle would appear odd to most, it became normal for us. And there was comfort in the community we found, a community that felt called to raise our children on mission for the glory of God.

And just to clarify, I'm not saying that mission is something you must go *out there* and do. As we saw with George Müller, mission can be right in front of us. Sometimes we simply need God to open our eyes. My point is this: God will either call you to live on mission in your community or he will bring community around you wherever he has called you to be on mission.

We just need to be open to the possibility that any new community may look different from the one we're used to. Remember, we're Christians—different is good!

We Have a Constant Companion

As we step away from normal into the unknown, we take God's Word with us as a compass, and we stick close to God's people as our community. But there is one more essential gift God has given us for our journey—himself. God is our constant companion. He is our steady, unchanging, faithful companion. (And yes, each of these gifts are words that begin with the letter *c*. This isn't because I am a supersavvy communicator but rather because, as the mother of four children, I need to keep things simple enough for me to remember them! Compass, community, and companion—it works for me!)

Have you ever noticed how many times the phrase "fear not," or a derivative of it, appears in the Bible? In both the Old and New Testaments, God is constantly calling his people out of a state of fear and anxiety. But the most notable thing about this charge is what accompanies it. He doesn't say, "Stop your crying and man up!" He doesn't call us to simply be braver, stronger, or more courageous. Throughout Scripture, we see the instruction to "fear not" followed by a promise: *I am with you.* Throughout the Old and New Testaments, these two phrases never cease to make an appearance hand in hand.

What I want to draw your attention to is not just the prominence of these two themes throughout Scripture but the relationship between them. There is a connectedness, one bolstering and empowering the other. Isaiah 41:10 says, "Fear not, for I am with you; be not dismayed, for I am your God; I will strengthen you, I will help you, I will uphold you with my righteous right hand." Joshua 1:9 tells us, "Be strong and courageous. Do not be frightened, and do not be dismayed, for the LORD your God is with you wherever you go." The Israelites were encouraged with these words: "Be strong and courageous. Do not fear or be in dread of [your enemies], for it is the LORD your God who goes with you. He will not leave you or forsake you" (Deut. 31:6).

Even in Jesus' last charge to his disciples, the send-off we refer to as the Great Commission, his command to them was daunting, but his final words gave them the assurance they needed for the task: "And behold, I am with you always, to the end of the age" (Matt. 28:20).

It is one thing to have a theoretical understanding of fear, and quite another to experience being gripped by fear or being freed from that grip. In the most basic sense, fear is a protective device God has given us to keep us from potentially dangerous situations. You may recall from your studies in psychology the fight-or-flight response. (By the way, I just exhausted my understanding of psychology, but I will press on.) The protective aspects of fear are genuine and important. Where it goes wrong is when fear becomes a longer-lasting response that creates anxiety and may even become debilitating. This is the fear I'm referencing with the admonition to "fear not."

Because we know God is true to his word, we have no need to fear, even when stepping into uncharted territory. The Lord is our constant companion. He was with Paul in every jail cell. He was with Daniel in the lion's den. He was with Jonah in the whale. The psalmist tells us there is no place we can go to escape his Spirit and nowhere to flee from his presence (Ps. 139:7). In a world in which very little remains constant, we can rest in the knowledge that our God will never leave us or forsake us.

He even sealed his commitment to us with the very blood of his Son. We may feel lonely, but we will never be alone. We may be abandoned by or estranged from people who promised to be constant, but our hearts are forever safe in the hands of a loving Father.

Lord Jesus, I'm Willing

This is where the adventure starts. It's accepting, however reluctantly, the invitation to climb up the tall tower, to face the fear of perilous heights, and take that first step off the platform. As I said before, it's not about having big faith but about having mustard-seed-sized faith in a big God. It's the man in Mark 9 who honestly responded to Jesus' call to faith with these all-too-familiar words: "I believe; help my unbelief!" (vv. 23–25). It's okay if you are not yet sure what mission should look like in your life, or if you are tentative about letting go of your home, self, identity, expectations, and security. All God is asking of you is to take that *first* step. I suggest it starts with these simple four words: *Lord Jesus, I'm willing.*

In closing, let me leave you with a song. In early fall 2020, I sat down with two of my songwriting buddies, Hank Bentley and Mia Fieldes. We chatted about how different everything looked in our pandemic days. Different for work, different for songwriting, different for touring, and different for raising kids. We talked honestly about what we missed—casually dropping in on neighbors, attending large gatherings without social distancing, and many other losses we'd been grieving.

What we discovered is that our loss of normal had us not in a place of disillusionment but in a place of expectancy. We spurred each other on to hope, and to dream big for the next season. We confessed our fears and trepidation over tours canceled and schools in limbo. And even though everything felt less settled and sturdy, we affirmed to each other how the unsteadiness of our circumstances had caused us to fall headlong into the waiting arms of our loving God.

In his hands, every loss has purpose. And every closed chapter marks the beginning of a new one, waiting to be written. May we say goodbye to normal with joy and expectation, believing that God has only the best in store for his children.

Hello, Unknown

I've grown accustomed to the way things are
I'm way more comfortable when it's familiar
I want a life where I can guard my heart
Cause easy is easy

I like the solid ground beneath my feet
The kind of road that someone else paved before me

I need a plan that both my eyes can see
But you call me to mystery

I am letting go
Of everything I've known
Farewell, predictable
No more playing it safe
I'll free fall into faith
I'll say goodbye, control
Hello, Unknown

I'm prone to find a way to skip the hard
The very trials you would use to refine me
There's beauty you create through every scar
If only I'm willing
Lord Jesus, I'm willing

What if I follow where you lead
What if the narrow road is steep
You know the plans you have for me
What if it's through the valley deep
What if it's only you and me
I still have everything I need
Jesus, you are everything I need[3]

It's Your Turn

I pray you've sensed my heart as I've shared the biblical principles and real-life stories that have helped me on my own journey in saying so long to normal. The families and individuals that you've read about are just regular folks I know—some from church, some through friends—who exhibit the kind of faith God has called us to, often in less-than-desirable situations. Each of these people would say that their story isn't necessarily extraordinary in and of itself, but that God has done and is doing extraordinary things *through* their story.

I share these stories not to wow you or to place any unrealistic expectations on you but to encourage you to dream big about your own story. It's not the greatness of our stories that makes them remarkable but the greatness of our God, seen throughout our stories.

In an effort to leave you with something concrete and applicable, I want to invite you to take this last step with me to make it personal. You may have noticed I used the same four questions in every interview I included in the book. Now it's your turn. I am asking you these same four core questions, but I've also included a few subquestions to help you dig a little deeper.

Clearly this assignment doesn't need to be turned in to a teacher or shared with your pastor, though you may find it personally helpful to share it with someone. The interview process is simply an opportunity to be honest with God and yourself, to take a personal inventory of your life and consider the ways God may be working that you maybe haven't recognized before.

My heartfelt prayer is that this personal interview will be yet one more step on your journey to confidently saying so long to normal and hello to God's glorious unknown!

1. **Describe the normal you used to know.**
   - What was your childhood like? Religious background? Previous view of God?
   - If you find yourself in a season of instability right now, can you identify a previous season that felt less shaky? Can you articulate what made that season feel more secure?
   - What feelings do you remember experiencing during that past season that you long to feel again?
2. **What happened in your life to bring you to the place of saying so long to normal?**
   - Using our definition of *trauma*—"any situation or event that adversely disrupts the normal routine of someone's life"—can you identify a traumatic event that caused a drifting or departure from the normal you used to know?
   - How have you experienced change in your relationships, vocation, or surroundings? Were these changes gradual or sudden?
   - What emotions accompanied this shift?
   - Grieving loss is an integral part of accepting change. Have you appropriately grieved the losses you have

experienced? Are there steps you need to take in fostering that grief?

3. **What has been your steady?**

- What has been your greatest source of comfort in the midst of life change? Can you identify key people, organizations, or practices that have helped you?
- How has your faith played a role in sustaining you? How has your church community been a help during this season?
- What are key promises of God or specific scriptures that have been your foundation during seasons of change? How has God's unchanging character comforted you?
- If faith, church, and Scripture haven't played a role in your season of transition, are there steps you need to take to change that reality? Do you have a church home, members of a faith community available to come alongside you, in good and hard seasons? Do you need further resources to help you understand how the truths of the Bible apply to your daily life?
- What are steps you can take today to trust God more fully with your life, rather than relying on your own strength and plans?

4. **What has been your gain?**

- How has God used change in your life to teach you something about yourself?
- How has God used change in your life to teach you something about *himself*?
- Joni Eareckson Tada has shared that a friend told her, "God uses what He hates to accomplish that which He loves."[1] How have you experienced this in your own life?
- What are blessings you can identify right now in your

life? What are daily choices you need to make that
would help you focus on your gain rather than become
embittered over your loss?

- How might maintaining a spiritual perspective improve
  your level of joy and peace, as well as enable you to be a
  greater blessing to those around you?

Acknowledgments

When I reflect on the creation of this project, the first word that comes to mind is *grateful*. I am so incredibly grateful for each person who contributed content, who lent their time proofreading, editing, or simply listening to me toss around ideas as I verbally separated the good from the ridiculous. To the friends who boldly shared their stories and countless others who made this book what it became, a thousand thank-yous.

To my Lord, Jesus Christ—thanks for using broken people and broken stories to accomplish immeasurably more than I could ask or imagine. May you be pleased with this offering, and may I be diligent to live out these truths, by your grace.

To Debbie Wickwire and the team at W Publishing Group and HarperCollins Christian—it's been about six years since we started working together, and I still feel like I've won the publishing-house lottery! You guys are excellent at what you do, and I appreciate your coming alongside me to share what God has laid on my heart!

To Perimeter Church—you have been the most gracious church home I could have ever dreamed of. A special thanks to Craig and the worship staff who prayed for this project and picked up any slack when I had to take days off to write. And to Sojourn—thank you for the adventure! It's a joy to be part of a team that feels like family!

To the five families who were bold enough to share their stories for this book—Davon and Tara Stack; Andy and Martha Cook; John, Whitney, Wylie, and Lola Roland; Kevin Chung; and Bailey Moody—God's hand of redemption is seen so clearly in and through your lives. Thanks for living out your faith with such boldness and vulnerability!

To Hanan Betancourt and Tom Keel—you guys know how to take sound, lights, and cameras and make them into ministry moments. Thanks for your hard work and your humble hearts!

To Leigh McLeroy—thanks for lending me your vision early on in this endeavor. Know that I am fully aware that any good writing in this book exists because of what I've learned from you!

To my family—Martin, Josie, Ben, Griffin, and Tim (and Dani)—thanks for letting Mommy spend so many hours in the basement on her computer, and for every night you made yourself a peanut-butter-and-jelly sandwich for dinner just so Mom could have a few more minutes writing. I know now that writing a book is a family endeavor, so I share this accomplishment with you too!

Lastly, there are two people I would like to leave my greatest thanks, without whom this book would surely not have come into existence.

To Nicole Owens, my manager and close friend of ten years—thanks for believing I could do this. Thanks for how well you have always handled every other facet of the ministry so that I can work in the gifting God has given me. Despite all my shenanigans, you have stayed with me, and I am forever grateful for you!

And to Bill Wood, my cowriter and friend—your kindness to our family is the epitome of persevering love and commitment. You have been our pastor in the truest sense of the word. And getting to write this book with you is a dream come true for me. Let's do it again soon!

Notes

The Truth About Normal

1. *The Oxford Pocket Dictionary of Current English*, s.v., "Normal," Encyclopedia.com, March 23, 2021, https://www.encyclopedia.com /places/united-states-and-canada/us-political-geography/normal.
2. Trenton Lott (staff devotion, Perimeter Church, Atlanta, GA, July 28, 2020).
3. Alexander Pope, *An Essay on Man: Moral Essays and Satires* (London: Cassell, 1891), epist. 1, sec. 3, line 19, https://www .gutenberg.org/files/2428/2428-h/2428-h.htm.

Chapter 1: Why We Crave Normal

1. Saint Augustine, *Confessions: A New Translation*, trans. Peter Constantine (New York: Liveright, 2018), 1.
2. Don Richardson, *Eternity in Their Hearts* (Ventura, CA: Regal Books, 1981), 103–4.
3. Joni Mitchell, "Woodstock," performed by Crosby, Stills, Nash, & Young, original release 1970, A&M Studios.

Chapter 2: The Shaking of What Can Be Shaken

1. Courtney Doctor, *Steadfast: A Devotional Bible Study on the Book of James* (Deerfield, IL: Gospel Coalition, 2019).
2. Edward Mote, "The Solid Rock" (public domain, 1834), https://hymnary .org/hymn/OLOF2018/113.

Chapter 3: So Long, Home

1. R. Alan Cole, *Exodus*, Tyndale Old Testament Commentaries (London: Inter-Varsity Press, 1973), 27, 28.

Chapter 4: So Long, Self

1. Timothy Keller, *The Freedom of Self-Forgetfulness: The Path to True Christian Joy* (Leyland, UK: 10Publishing, 2012), 32.
2. MercyMe, "So Long Self," written by Bart Millard (Brentwood, TN: INO Records, 2006).
3. *Talladega Nights*, directed by Adam McKay (Culver City, CA: Columbia Pictures, 2006).
4. Ray Ortlund, *The Gospel: How the Church Portrays the Beauty of Christ* (Wheaton, IL: Crossway, 2014), 15.
5. Randy Pope, *The Answer: Putting an End to the Search for Life Satisfaction* (Duluth, GA: Life-on-Life Resources, 2005), 30.
6. Pope, *The Answer*, 29–38.
7. Keller, *The Freedom of Self-Forgetfulness*, 39.
8. Elyse M. Fitzpatrick, *Because He Loves Me: How Christ Transforms Our Daily Life* (Wheaton, IL: Crossway, 2008), 25.
9. E. E. Hewitt, "My Faith Has Found a Resting Place" (public domain, 1891).

Chapter 5: So Long, Identity

1. Bruce J. Malina, *The New Testament World: Insights from Cultural Anthropology*, 3rd ed. (Louisville, KY: Westminster John Knox, 2001), 144.

Chapter 6: So Long, Expectations

1. Leon Morris, *Luke: An Introduction and Commentary*, vol. 3, Tyndale New Testament Commentaries (Grand Rapids, MI: Eerdmans, 1988), 91.
2. C. S. Lewis, *The Weight of Glory* (New York: HarperOne, 2001), 26.
3. Morris, *Luke*, 92.
4. John Stott, with Dale Larsen and Sandy Larsen, *Reading Romans with John Stott*, vol. 2 (Downers Grove, IL: InterVarsity Press, 2016), 113.

Chapter 7: So Long, Security

1. Dean R. Ulrich, *From Famine to Fullness: The Gospel According to Ruth* (Phillipsburg, NJ: P&R Publishing, 2007), 29.
2. Martin Luther, *Explanation of the Lord's Prayer*, Sixth Petition ("And lead us not into temptation"), par. 161, https://christianity .stackexchange.com/questions/68678/where-did-martin-luther-say.
3. Larry Crabb, *Fully Alive* (Grand Rapids, MI: Baker, 2013), 111.
4. John Piper, quoting 2 Corinthians 3:18, in *God Is the Gospel* (Wheaton, IL: Crossway, 2005), 93.

Chapter 8: Hello, New Life

1. Paul David Tripp, *New Morning Mercies: A Daily Devotional* (Wheaton, IL: Crossway, 2014), s.v. "September 23."
2. Jessi Alexander and Jon Mabe, "The Climb," performed by Miley Cyrus (Hollywood Records/Walt Disney Records, 2009).
3. Andrew Murray, *Abide in Christ* in *Andrew Murray on Prayer* (New Kensington, PA: Whitaker House, 1979), 25, italics added.
4. Murray, *Abide in Christ*, 25.
5. George William Cooke, "Joy in My Heart," copyright 1925.
6. Renee Taft Meloche, *George Müller: Faith to Feed Ten Thousand* (Seattle: YWAM Publishing, 2001).
7. George Müller, *A Narrative of Some of the Lord's Dealings with George Müller* (London: J. Nisbet, 1855), 48.
8. D. G. Amphlett, *The Bristol Book of Days* (Gloucestershire, UK: History Press, 2011), s.v. "April 20th."

Chapter 9: Hello, New Vision

1. Jon Bloom, "You Are Not Your Own," *Desiring God* (blog), January 22, 2019, https://www.desiringgod.org/articles/you-are-not-your-own.
2. John Phillips, *Exploring the Gospel of Matthew: An Expository Commentary*, The John Phillips Commentary Series (Grand Rapids, MI: Kregel, 1999), 174.
3. Arthur Bennett, ed., *The Valley of Vision: A Collection of Puritan Prayers and Devotions* (Carlisle, PA: Banner of Truth Trust, 1975), 177.

Chapter 10: Hello, New Mission

1. *Mission: Impossible—Rogue Nation*, directed by Christopher McQuarrie (Hollywood: Paramount Pictures, 2015).

2. Jean Fleming, *Between Walden and the Whirlwind* (Colorado Springs: NavPress, 1986), 13–14.

3. Though if you read the story of Jonah, you might quickly agree that he was more reluctant than Moses and for reasons unlike Moses' reasons.

4. Judges 6:36–40.

5. Isaiah 6:1–8.

6. Jeremiah 1:4–19.

7. Matthew 28:16–20.

8. Derek W. H. Thomas, *Heaven on Earth: What the Bible Teaches About Life to Come* (Ross-shire, Scotland: Christian Focus Publications, 2018), 110–11.

9. Dane C. Ortlund, *Gentle and Lowly: The Heart of Christ for Sinners and Sufferers* (Wheaton, IL: Crossway, 2020), 184. Ephesians 2:7 reads, ". . . so that in the coming ages he might show the immeasurable riches of his grace in kindness toward us in Christ Jesus."

Chapter 11: Hello, Unknown

1. "Wherever He Leads I'll Go," in Robert J. Morgan, *Near to the Heart of God: Meditations on 366 Best-Loved Hymns* (Grand Rapids, MI: Revell, 2010), s.v. "January 17."

2. Wayne A. Grudem, *1 Peter*, vol. 17, Tyndale New Testament Commentaries (Grand Rapids, MI: Eerdmans, 1988), 81.

3. Hank Bentley, Mia Fields, and Laura Story, "Hello, Unknown," 2021. Copyright © 2021 Every Square Inch (SESAC) Capitol CMG Amplifier (SESAC) (adm. at CapitolCMGPublishing.com). All rights reserved. Used by permission. Copyright © 2021 Upside Down Under (BMI) / Be Essential Songs (BMI) / (admin at EssentialMusicPublishing.com). All rights reserved. Used by permission. Copyright © 2021 Laura's Stories and Songs (ASCAP) / (admin at musicservices.org). All rights reserved. Used by permission.

It's Your Turn

1. Joni Eareckson Tada, "God Permits What He Hates," *Joni & Friends* (podcast), May 15, 2013, https://old.joniandfriends.org/radio/4 -minute/god-permits-what-he-hates1/.

About the Author

Laura Story is a wife, mother, songwriter, worship leader, author, artist, and Bible teacher. Her songs—which have won Grammys, Billboard Music Awards, and Dove Awards—include "Blessings," "Mighty to Save," and Chris Tomlin's "Indescribable." Laura has a master's degree in theological studies and a doctorate in worship studies, and has served as a worship leader at Perimeter Church in Atlanta since 2005. Her greatest joy is being a wife to Martin and mother to Josie, Ben, Griffin, and Timothy.

New Video Study for Your Church or Small Group

If you've enjoyed this book, now you can go deeper with the companion video Bible study!

In this five-session study, Laura Story helps you apply the principles in *So Long, Normal* to your life. The study guide includes streaming video access, video teaching notes, group discussion questions, personal reflection questions, and a leader's guide.

Study Guide with
Streaming Video
9780310142317

DVD
9780310142331

Available now at your favorite bookstore,
or streaming video on StudyGateway.com.

Also by Laura Story

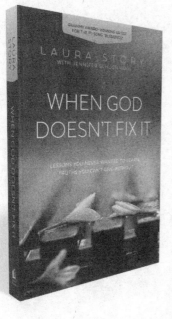

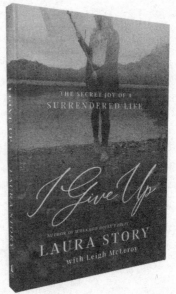

Available wherever books and ebooks are sold

Check out Laura's music!

Available wherever music is sold.